Maria
Shrines

263   92,167
Czarnopys, Theresa Santa
Marian shrines of the United States:
  a pilgrim's travel guide

DATE DUE   13.95

DISCARD

Marian Shrines
OF THE
United States

◆ *A Pilgrim's Travel Guide* ◆

Theresa Santa Czarnopys and
Rev. Thomas M. Santa, C.Ss.R.

Liguori
LIGUORI, MISSOURI

Library of Congress Cataloging-in-Publication Data

Czarnopys, Theresa Santa, 1954–
    Marian shrines of the United States : a pilgrim's travel guide / Theresa Santa Czarnopys and Thomas M. Santa. — 1st ed.
        p. cm.
    Includes index.
    ISBN 0-7648-0227-5
    1. Mary, Blessed Virgin, Saint—Shrines—United States—Guidebooks. 2. Christian pilgrims and pilgrimages—United States—Guidebooks. 3. United States—Guidebooks. I. Santa, Thomas M., 1952– . II. Title
BT652.U6C83 1998
263'.04273—dc21   98-20164

Printed in the United States of America
02 01 00 99 98   5 4 3 2 1
First Edition

In loving memory of our grandmother Margaret Driscoll and our aunt Mary Margaret (Driscoll) Sketch, and in grateful thanks to our mother, Joan Ellen (Driscoll) Santa, we dedicate this effort. These three strong, beautiful, and devout women are the inspiration behind this book.

CONTENTS

INTRODUCTION

"The family that prays together stays together."

We were children of the fifties, born into a German-Irish Catholic family, the children of a mother and a grandmother who had great devotion to our Blessed Mother. Our home always had a picture of the Blessed Mother prominently displayed, and there were numerous statues of Mary throughout the house. It seemed to us that all of our flowerpots and planters were, in fact, statues of Mary, with the planter or vase attached! Our family car displayed a medallion of Our Lady of the Highways, along with one of Saint Christopher, and we wore the appropriate scapular medals around our necks. In this we were probably not different from most Catholic families of the time.

We were also members of a Catholic parish community, staffed by the Redemptorist Fathers and Brothers, a religious community with a strong devotion to our Blessed Mother under the title of Our Mother of Perpetual Help. This particular devotion was expressed with special prayers and novena services every Tuesday and with a special nine-day novena once a year, usually during the month of October. Our mother made sure that we were present for all scheduled devotions, and although we have not continued to express our devotion in this way, our mother continues to do so with great enthusiasm and dedication.

The Dominican Sisters who staffed our parish school, not to be outdone by the Redemptorists and their particular devotion, enabled and promoted the tradition of the May crowning of the Blessed Mother. Each year, on the designated day, the entire school gathered in the front yard of the convent and spilled out into the street and parking lots as the statue of Mary was crowned. It was considered a great honor to be chosen as the student representative who actually placed the crown of flowers upon the statue's head. Neither of us was ever chosen for this honor, but if asked, we would have eagerly accepted.

The formative years of our lives were marked by obvious devotion to Mary; however, later, especially after the reforms of the Second Vatican Council, our devotion became much less obvious and even a little restrained. We experienced a significant change, as did most other Catholics, as the prayers and devotions that were once so central to our Catholic lives became less and less pronounced. The change in our practice was not something that we consciously chose but was rather a slow erosion, hardly noticed and certainly not missed until much later in our lives.

Today, some forty years after the experience of our youth, we can discover the most obvious expressions of devotion to the Blessed Mother demonstrated on two distinct occasions: at death and at the nuptial Mass.

A practice still continues for the newly married couple to bring fresh flowers to the Marian altar and shrine in the church and to pray for Mary's blessing on the union just celebrated. This is a practice that both of us incorporated into our sacramental celebrations, Theresa's wedding and Tom's first Mass of Ordination. Neither of us needed to be prompted to choose this expression of devotion, and it was accepted and expected by the congregation that had gathered with us to celebrate.

The Catholic wake, the service that normally takes place before the funeral Mass, still includes the praying of the rosary, either as the central prayer for the deceased person or, as is now more often the case, as a private expression of sympathy, prayed by the many who are gathered. It is very common for the deceased to be holding a rosary in their folded hands, which they will take to their grave in the hopes that Mary will not forget them, "now and at the hour of our death."

Other devotional practices to Mary still find appropriate expressions in Catholic life. It is not a surprise to discover a statue of Mary in the family garden or to discover an old upturned and half-buried bathtub that will serve as a family "grotto" or "shrine." Certainly, pictures of our Blessed Mother and holy cards are still prominent in Catholic life, and the rosary remains a traditional gift for first Communion.

In the pages that follow we have collected a representative sampling of the public shrines, grottoes, and places of pilgrimage to the Blessed Mother that exist in the United States. In one sense, this collection of places is a reflection of our historical past; most of the shrines and places of devotion were constructed and dedicated many years ago. However, in another sense, they are representative of a lively devotion to Mary that continues today—these are not places that are deserted but are, rather, places of life and vibrancy.

We have not included every shrine and grotto of importance or even those lesser-known places of devotion that hold a special place in our hearts. We include only those places that cooperated with us in our research and visitations; some places that we wanted to include in our collection declined our invitation.

It will surely be observed that the East Coast of the United States and the Midwest seem to dominate our work. The West Coast and the Southwest seem to be barely mentioned or noted. There are two reasons for this—and these are not, as may be assumed, reflective of a lack of effort or interest on our part. The first reason is that most of the shrines and grottoes to Our Lady seem to be the visible expressions of a national or immigrant church, and until very recently this phenomena was expressed most often in the eastern and midwestern states. By the time further westward movement took place, there did not seem to be a pronounced need to express devotion to Mary, as had been the earlier tradition. The second reason clarifies and expands the first. Westward expansion in the United States discovered a tradition of devotion to Mary, under the title of Our Lady of Guadalupe, that permeated Catholic faith and practice. There was no need to erect a special shrine or place of devotion since all places were centers for devotion already. Every church, monastery, and mission station enshrined at least a picture of Our Lady of Guadalupe.

How to Use This Book

We envision that most of the people who read this book will most likely not travel to the places that are presented. It is a phenomenon of travel books that the people who read them prefer to "travel" to the places presented in their imaginations, rather than by plane, train, or automobile. With this in mind, we made every attempt to provide the reader with enough information to enjoy their pilgrimage without the need to leave the comfort of their living room.

For those who read this book for the purpose of actually visiting the places presented, it is our assumption that the vast majority will do so by car or public transport—and we made every effort to be as clear as we could be with our directions. They are clear to us, but we admit that we might have missed something in the telling! We apologize in advance for any inconvenience.

We would suggest that a good home for this book, after a first review, might not be your bookcase but rather the glove compartment of your car. Who knows when you might find yourself within a reasonable driving distance of a shrine or grotto or place of pilgrimage that might make your trip into something truly memorable?

God bless each of you, and may our Blessed Mother watch over you and guide you.

Northeast Region

Basilica of the National Shrine of the Assumption of the Blessed Virgin Mary

BALTIMORE, MARYLAND

The Basilica of the National Shrine of the Assumption of the Blessed Virgin Mary is the embodiment of the vision of the first bishop (later archbishop) of the United States, John Carroll. Consecrated in 1790 at the chapel at Lulworth Castle in England, Bishop Carroll recognized from the beginning of his work that St. Peter's Mass House on Saratoga Street, the "Pro-Cathedral," was inadequate and "paltry" for the first see in the United States. Thus, when the Holy Father wrote him, urging that he "erect a church in the form of a cathedral, in as much as the times and circumstances allow," Bishop Carroll began the long process of building this great church, naming it in honor of the Assumption of the Virgin Mary. At his episcopal consecration on the Feast of the Assumption in 1790, he designated Our Lady as the patroness of the United States, making that day the principal feast of the new diocese.

The interior of the Basilica of the National Shrine of the Assumption of the Blessed Virgin Mary. It is considered one of the finest examples of nineteenth-century architecture in the world. *(Basilica of the National Shrine of the Assumption of the Blessed Virgin Mary)*

PRAYER INVOKING THE INTERCESSION OF MARY

Almighty God, you gave a humble virgin the privilege of being the Mother of your Son, and crowned her with the glory of heaven. May the prayers of the Virgin Mary bring us to the salvation of Christ and raise us up to eternal life.

FROM THE FEAST OF THE ASSUMPTION OF MARY

ABOUT THE SHRINE

Benjamin Henry Latrobe, architect of the U.S. Capitol, designed the basilica with a neoclassical design inspired by buildings in London, Paris, and Dorchester, England. The traditional cruciform church with a domed crossing is recognizable, but his main dome was expanded to embrace almost the whole church. The choir and transepts have been recessed, and the nave is reduced to a two-bay vestibule. All these open into the central domed space by segmental arches, with smaller semicircular arches between them. The rotunda (actually a circle within an octagon within a square) offers an interesting study in design and measurement. Its four great supporting piers rest upon inverted arches in the undercroft, through which the weight of the foundation is equalized. When this cathedral was dedicated on May 31, 1821, it was one of the most architecturally original cathedrals in the world and heralded a "new movement" in cathedral building. Today it is considered one of the finest nineteenth-century buildings in the world and Latrobe's masterpiece.

SHRINE INFORMATION

Basilica of the National Shrine of the Assumption of the Blessed Virgin Mary
408 North Charles Street
Baltimore, MD 21201
(410) 727-3564
fax: (410) 539-0407

TOURIST INFORMATION

Specific information regarding restaurants and hotel/motel facilities can be obtained by writing to the above address.

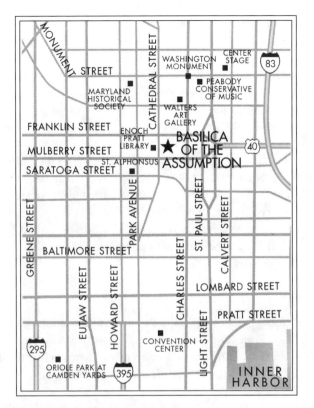

DIRECTIONS TO THE SHRINE

The basilica, located in downtown Baltimore, is easily accessible by car or bus. You can also use Ed Kane's Water Taxi & Trolley System from Baltimore's Inner Harbor, or you can take the short walk north on Charles Street from the Inner Harbor to the Mount Vernon District. Parking is available on the street and in the Franklin Street Garage located between Charles and Cathedral Streets. Parking in the garage is free on Sundays between 7:00 A.M. and 1:00 P.M., and from 3:00 P.M. until 7:00 P.M. At all others times the garage charges a fee.

FOR FIRST-TIME PILGRIMS

The Basilica of the National Shrine of the Assumption of the Blessed Virgin Mary is open Monday through Friday from 7:00 A.M. until 5:00 P.M. and on weekends from 7:00 A.M. until 6:30 P.M. The basilica offers guided tours every Sunday after the 10:45 A.M. Mass (tours begin at approximately noon). The tours cover the construction and building of the cathedral and the development and growth of Catholicism in the United States. Private tours are also available by appointment. There is no fee for tours, but donations are appreciated.

It is important to a great majority of visitors, national and international, to be able to attend a liturgy at the basilica. Masses are celebrated weekdays at 7:30 A.M. and 12:10 P.M. and on Saturday at 7:30 A.M. and 5:30 P.M. (vigil). Sunday Mass is scheduled at 7:30, 9:00 (Latin Mass), and 10:45 A.M. (choir) and at 4:00 and 5:30 P.M. Eucharistic adoration is every Friday from 12:30 P.M. until 3:45 P.M., and public recitation of the rosary is every Saturday at 5:00 P.M.

Also available to pilgrims is the Basilica Museum Shop featuring religious articles and basilica memorabilia; the shop is located below the basilica sacristy.

OF SPECIAL INTEREST

On October 8, 1995, the basilica was greatly honored with a visit by His Holiness Pope John Paul II, during his historic visit to Baltimore. While in the basilica, he prayed for several moments before the Blessed Sacrament and then took in the rich history represented by the cathedral.

On May 29, 1996, Mother Teresa of Calcutta received the Renewal of Vows from thirty-five of her Missionary of Charity Sisters in the basilica. An estimated 1,400 people attended the Mass, concelebrated by William Cardinal Keeler and about 40 priests of the Archdiocese of Baltimore. Hundreds of volunteers and friends of the Missionaries of Charity, as well as more than 70 Missionaries of Charity Sisters, were among the congregation. The Basilica and Santo Niño Choirs performed the liturgical music together.

Basilica of the National Shrine of the Immaculate Conception

WASHINGTON, D.C.

In 1847, at the petition of the American bishops, Pope Pius IX named Mary, under the title of her Immaculate Conception, as patroness of the United States. Then in the early 1900s Bishop Thomas J. Shahan, the fourth rector of the Catholic University of America in Washington, D.C., suggested building a shrine to Mary adjacent to the university campus. Bishop Shahan presented his plan to Pope Pius X in a special audience and received not only a $400 personal contribution from the pontiff but his enthusiastic support as well. In 1913 the Board of Trustees of the Catholic University of America agreed to donate a parcel of land on which would be built the National Shrine of the Immaculate Conception.

The Basilica of the National Shrine of the Immaculate Conception stands majestically in the capital city as a spiritual center for the nation. *(Basilica of the National Shrine of the Immaculate Conception)*

PRAYER TO OUR LADY

O Lady, showered with praise and blessing above all creatures! You are the only Mother of God, the Queen of the Universe, the dispenser of all graces, the ornament of the Church; in you is contained the incomprehensible greatness of all virtues, of all gifts. You are the temple of God, the paradise of delight, the model of all the just, the consolation of your people, the glory and the source of salvation; you are the gate of heaven, the joy of the elect, the

*object of God's affection. It is only imperfectly that we can cel-
ebrate your praises. We beg you to make up for our deficiencies
so that we may praise you throughout eternity. Amen.*
SAINT BERNARDINE OF SIENA

ABOUT THE SHRINE

The Basilica of the National Shrine of the Immaculate Conception
is a marvelous place of prayer and pilgrimage. Every chapel and hall-
way reverberates with the presence of the sacred. From the hallowed
names of the hundreds of generous benefactors engraved in Memorial
Hall, to the serenity of the penance chapel, to the majestic beauty of
the Great Upper Church, to the silent intimacy of the Blessed Sacrament Chapel, the presence of God permeates this magnificent sanctuary. It is the realization of Bishop Shahan's dream of a "great hymn in
stone."

In the center of the Crypt Church is the exquisitely carved Mary's
Altar dedicated to Our Lady of the Catacombs. The altar was a gift to
the National Shrine from more than thirty thousand women named
Mary and has been used for the celebration of Mass since 1927. The
Great Upper Church of the Shrine was added in 1954, and in the decades that followed many chapels were added, each reflecting the
religious heritage brought to America by generations of immigrant
Catholics. These chapels represent both the diversity of Catholic faith
and the strength of unity achieved through devotion to Our Lady.
Stained glass, mosaic, and sculpture serve to record this rich and vibrant heritage of prayer and devotion.

The basilica represents nearly a century of fervent faith, devotion,
and generosity on the part of American Catholics. As a spiritual center
for the nation, the shrine stands majestically in the capital city as a
constant reminder of Mary's perfect response to the Lord: "Let it be
done to me according to thy will."

Each year more than a half million pilgrims, united in their devotion to the Blessed Virgin Mary, journey to this sacred shrine to worship her Son and our Savior Jesus Christ.

SHRINE INFORMATION

Basilica of the National Shrine of the Immaculate Conception
400 Michigan Avenue, NE
Washington, D.C. 20017
(202) 526-8300
website: www.nationalshrine.com
e-mail: shrine@cris.com

TOURIST INFORMATION

Restaurants and hotel accommodations are readily available in the immediate area. The shrine has its own dining room, which is open daily from 8:30 A.M.

DIRECTIONS TO THE SHRINE

The Basilica of the National Shrine of the Immaculate Conception is located in the northeastern quadrant of Washington, D.C., next to Catholic University. The easiest way to get to the shrine is to take the Metrorail's Red Line, and get off at the Brookland/CUA stop.

FOR FIRST-TIME PILGRIMS

The basilica can be slightly overwhelming to the first-time visitor, but thankfully there are guided tours available each day, and a very helpful welcoming booklet is available to all visitors. A suggested strategy for your visit would be to enter the basilica, secure a copy of the welcoming booklet, and find a comfortable pew in the upper church to sit down and gather your thoughts. After a few minutes of private prayer, you can review the booklet, highlighting the chapels that are of particular interest to you.

For the pilgrim with a special devotion to the Blessed Mother, the basilica is a unique opportunity to experience her as she is known under several titles. Chapels to our Blessed Mother under her various titles can be found in both the crypt level of the basilica and the great upper church. A listing follows:

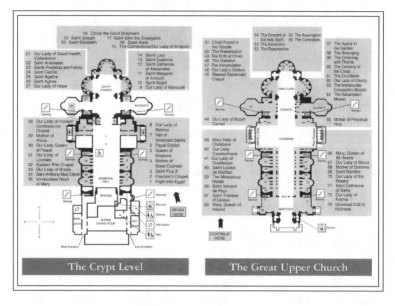

- The Crypt Level: Mother of Good Counsel; Queen of Missions; Our Lady of Bistrica; Our Lady of Hostyn; Our Lady, Queen of Peace; Our Lady of Lourdes; Our Lady of Brezje; and Immaculate Heart of Mary.
- The Great Upper Church: Our Lady, Queen of Ireland; Our Lady of Guadalupe; Our Lady of Czestochowa; Mary, Help of Christians; Our Lady of Mount Carmel; Our Lady of Charity; Mother of Perpetual Help; Mary, Queen of All Hearts; Our Lady of Siluva; Mother of Sorrows; Our Lady of the Rosary; and Our Lady of Fátima.

The Basilica of the National Shrine of the Immaculate Conception is open November 1–March 31 from 7:00 A.M.–6:00 P.M. and April 1–October 31 from 7:00 A.M.–7:00 P.M.

Mass is celebrated daily in the Crypt Church at 7:00, 7:30, 8:00, and 8:30 A.M., 12:10 and 5:15 P.M., as well as on Sundays at 7:30 A.M. and 1:30 P.M. (Latin Mass). Mass is celebrated in the Great Upper Church at 9:00 and 10:30 A.M., noon, and 4:30 P.M. on Sundays only. Holy Days and Christmas, January 1, and Easter have special Mass schedules.

Every day of the week, at various times of the day, pilgrims are invited to share in the rosary and the sacrament of reconciliation.

Guided tours of the shrine are offered daily and on Sundays; however, group tours are by special arrangement. A gift shop and bookstore on the Crypt Level are also open to pilgrims. The shrine is completely handicapped accessible.

OF SPECIAL INTEREST

The Basilica of the National Shrine of the Immaculate Conception, impressive in its tremendous size and beauty, tells the story of the faith of countless generations of American Catholics whose descendants brought their heritage of Christianity to America on the waves of immigration. It has no parish community, no single bishop claims it as his cathedral, and it is not supported by a single group or organization. Located as it is in our nation's capital, it is best understood as America's Church. A visit to the basilica is an experience of "coming home."

Basilica of Our Lady of Perpetual Help
MISSION CHURCH,
REDEMPTORIST FATHERS AND BROTHERS
BOSTON, MASSACHUSETTS

In 1832, exactly one hundred years after the founding of the Congregation of the Most Holy Redeemer in the Kingdom of Naples in 1732, the first overseas mission of the Redemptorists was launched. Three of the Redemptorist Fathers and three Brothers came to America. The first seven years were a time of struggle and insecurity. These Redemptorists were scattered, working among the Indians in the Northwest Territory of Wisconsin and Michigan and among the German immigrants in northern Ohio. But in 1839 they secured their first permanent foundation in Pittsburgh, a church in a converted factory building. The superior of the Redemptorists in America at that time was Fr. Joseph Prost, and he made this remarkable statement: "I have no doubt that our Congregation of Redemptorists was called to America to spread devotion to the Blessed Virgin."

In 1869, just thirty-nine years after the first permanent foundation in Pittsburgh, Bishop John Joseph Williams invited the Redemptorists to Boston, where they purchased the Brinley House and estate of five acres in Roxbury. Rich in Revolutionary War history, the Brinley House was one of the places where the idea of the Declaration of Independence was first advanced. On January 29, 1871, the first church, a wooden structure, was built and dedicated to Our Lady of Perpetual Help. The picture of Our Lady of Perpetual Help, entrusted to the Redemptorists by Pope Pius IX, who told them to "make her known," was solemnly enthroned above the main altar. Destroyed by fire in 1876, the old church was rebuilt, and a special shrine was built for Our Lady of Perpetual Help.

PRAYER TO OUR LADY OF PERPETUAL HELP

Mother of Perpetual Help, you have been blessed and favored by God. You became not only the Mother of the Redeemer, but the mother of the redeemed as well. We come to you today as your loving children. Watch over us and take care of us. As you held the child Jesus in your loving arms, so take us in your arms. Be a mother ready at every moment to help us. For God who is mighty has done great things for you, and his mercy is from age to age on those who love him. Our greatest fear is that in time of temptation we may fail to call on you, and become lost children. Intercede for us, dear Mother, in obtaining pardon for our sins, love for Jesus, final perseverance, and the grace always to call upon you. Amen.

ABOUT THE SHRINE

The picture of Our Lady of Perpetual Help is the heart of the shrine, where prayers have been going up and favors have been coming down for more than a century. Crutches at the shrine are testimony to some of the cures that have been documented from among the huge crowds of people who have attended the Blessing of the Sick. Beneath the picture of Our Lady of Perpetual Help is a picture of Saint Alphonsus Liguori, whose devotion to the Blessed Mother resulted in the founding of the Redemptorists, his spiritual sons whose zeal for Mary, the Mother of God, is carried with them wherever they go.

SHRINE INFORMATION

Redemptorist Fathers and Brothers
Mission Church
1545 Tremont Street
Boston, MA 02120
(617) 445-2600

TOURIST INFORMATION

Restaurant and hotel accommodations are readily available in the nearby downtown area.

DIRECTIONS TO THE SHRINE

The Basilica of Our Lady of Perpetual Help is located in downtown Boston, not far from the New City Hall.

FROM THE SOUTH ON I-95

Take I-95 north, then head east on Rte. 128/I-93 and take 3/I-93 north to downtown Boston. Stay in the left lane until you see the Mass. Ave./Roxbury exit. *At the end of the ramp go straight through eight sets of lights (you are on Melnea Cass Boulevard). At the ninth set of lights, take a left onto Tremont Street. Travel through four sets of lights, and Tremont St. goes right. Drive approximately a quarter mile, and the church is on the right.

FROM THE MASSACHUSETTS TURNPIKE

Head east on the Massachusetts Turnpike (I-90) and take I-93 south to the Mass. Ave./Roxbury exit. Follow the directions at * just above.

FROM THE NORTH

Take Rte. 128/I-95 south, then take Rte. 9 east toward Boston. Stay on Rte. 9 until the very end. Come to Brookline Village and go under the bridge to the lights at South Huntington Avenue. Go straight. This road turns into Huntington Avenue. Follow Huntington Avenue for a quarter mile. Pass two sets of lights and come to the lights at Brigham Circle. Tremont Street will be on the right-hand side. The church is two blocks up on the left.

FROM THE SOUTH SHORE/CAPE COD

Take the Rte. 3/I-93 (Southeast Expressway) north toward downtown Boston, exiting onto the Mass. Ave./Roxbury exit. Follow the directions at * above.

FROM DOWNTOWN CROSSING

Take the Orange Line Subway Train, which runs from Oak Grove in Malden to Forest Hills. Get off at Roxbury Crossing. The basilica is three blocks up on the right-hand side.

FROM PARK STREET

Take the Green Line trolley, which runs from Lechmere in Cambridge to Heath Street in Jamaica Plain. Get off at Brigham Circle. The basilica is three blocks up on the left-hand side.

FROM THE AIRPORT

On the subway, take the Green Line E train to Brigham Circle, several blocks west on Tremont Street.

FOR FIRST-TIME PILGRIMS

Novena services are held every Wednesday at 9:00 A.M., 12:10, 5:30, and 7:30 P.M. Spanish novena is held at 6:30 P.M.

A PILGRIM'S PROMISE

During the blessed half hour of the novena, you will find that care slips from your shoulders like a heavy sack, and peace pours in like sunlight through the windows of your soul because the shrine is a hallowed spot, chosen by Mary herself for reasons no one can say. What many pilgrims can tell you, though, is that on every Wednesday, angels pass one another on unseen golden ladders above the shrine, carrying urgent petitions up, bringing merciful answers down. For Mary still is what she called herself centuries ago, the Mother of Perpetual Help.

Boatmen's Shrine of Our Lady of the Hudson

PRESENTATION CHURCH
PORT EWEN, NEW YORK

Port Ewen, New York, was settled in 1841 primarily to handle the coal from Pennsylvania that was being transported to northern markets via the Delaware-Hudson Canal. The towing companies, the International Longshoremen's Association, and families whose members had been boatmen for generations conceived and financed the Boatmen's Shrine of Our Lady of the Hudson, in commemoration of the hundreds of men whose entire lives were spent working the waterways from New York City to the Great Lakes. The sculptor Thomas Penning of Woodstock, New York, carved a six-foot statue of Our Blessed Lady, who is holding a symbolic tugboat in her arm, from ageless bluestone native to the area. The statue, dedicated on June 28, 1952, was unveiled by Mrs. Patrick Hines, mother of five sons, all tugboatmen.

Boatmen's Shrine of Our Lady of the Hudson was established to give thanks to the Blessed Virgin for the safety of the hundreds of men whose entire lives were spent working the waterways from New York City to the Great Lakes. *(Anthony F. Chiffolo)*

PRAYER TO THE MOTHER OF OUR REDEEMER

Loving Mother of the Redeemer, gate of heaven, star of the sea, assist your people who have fallen yet strive to rise again. To the wonderment of nature you bore your creator, yet remained a virgin as before. You who received Gabriel's joyful greeting, have pity on us poor sinners. Amen.

ABOUT THE SHRINE

The Boatmen's Shrine of Our Lady of the Hudson is located on the grounds of the Church of the Presentation of the Blessed Virgin at Port Ewen. In addition to the statue of Our Blessed Lady, the grounds include a set of metal Stations of the Cross donated by the "boatmen," who also presented the parish with gifts of land.

SHRINE INFORMATION

Presentation Church
Box 904
Father Kelley Drive
Port Ewen, NY 12466

TOURIST INFORMATION

Restaurant and hotel accommodations are available in the nearby towns of Kingston to the north and New Paltz to the south.

DIRECTIONS TO THE SHRINE

Port Ewen is on the western side of the Hudson River, approximately one hundred miles north of New York City. It is easily accessed by car using the New York State Thruway system: exit at Kingston if coming from the north and New Paltz if coming from the south. Proceed to Route 9W. Presentation Church and the Boatmen's Shrine is approximately halfway between the Kingston and New Paltz Thruway exits. Once in Port Ewen, turn down East Main Street toward the Hudson River. The church is on the right two blocks down and is easy to find.

FOR FIRST-TIME PILGRIMS

It might be a bit of a trip to make a special pilgrimage to the Shrine of Our Lady of the Hudson, but it is well worth a detour if you find yourself in the general area. A trip on Route 9W is interesting because it is home to many religious orders that constructed their seminaries and monasteries in the early 1900s. On a stretch of 9W between Esopus and New Paltz, you will pass the Marianists, the Redemptorists, the Christian Brothers, the Cabrini Sisters, and the Episcopal Monastery of the Holy Cross. Mount Saint Alphonsus, the former theologate of the Redemptorist Community, dominates the geography of the area. A massive granite structure, it rises majestically on the banks of the Hudson. If you stand on the front steps of the seminary and look across the Hudson River to the south, it is possible to identify historical structures of a not-too-distant past: the home of President Franklin Roosevelt and the summer home of Cornelius Vanderbilt. The experience serves as a nice contrast.

OF SPECIAL INTEREST

The seminary chapel of Mount Saint Alphonsus is the chapel where hundreds of men have been ordained and sent forth for ministry throughout the world. The chapel features a special side altar in honor of Our Mother of Perpetual Help. If you kneel at the altar in the place where hundreds have knelt before, you can almost hear the prayers of petition and thanks that have filled this sacred space.

$$\begin{array}{c|c} + & + \\ \hline + & + \end{array}$$

Central Shrine of Our Lady of the Miraculous Medal

ST. VINCENT'S SEMINARY
PHILADELPHIA, PENNSYLVANIA

Mary's Central Shrine is housed in the Chapel of the Immaculate Conception at St. Vincent's Seminary in Germantown, Philadelphia, Pennsylvania. It is the heart and center of devotion to Mary Immaculate under the title of Our Lady of the Miraculous Medal. It was here, in 1930, that the Miraculous Medal perpetual novena was started, with one service every Monday. Now there are twelve services attended by more than 10,000 people every Monday, and the perpetual novena has spread to more than 4,200 churches in this country and abroad.

In 1912 Fr. Joseph Skelly, C.M., was released from his seminary duties to devote his time to raising funds for the building of a new seminary to be located outside Princeton, New Jersey. He enclosed a miraculous medal in each fund-raising letter he sent out. The response was so great that Father Skelly felt that some special mark of gratitude to Mary was in order.

After much prayer and consultation, it was decided to form, in March, 1915, the Central Association of the Miraculous Medal, a pious association devoted to Mary's interests. The primary purpose of the Central Association was, and continues to be, the spreading of devotion to Mary Immaculate through her Miraculous Medal. Through the years, literally millions and millions of Miraculous Medals and booklets telling the story of the Miraculous Medal and containing the novena prayers have been distributed throughout the United States and abroad.

The Shrine of Our Lady of the Miraculous Medal—or, as it is commonly called, Mary's Central Shrine—was built in 1927. From then until 1930, four solemn novenas in honor of Our Lady of the Miraculous Medal were held annually. On December 8, 1930, the perpetual novena was initiated. Father Skelly started the perpetual novena as a way of celebrating the one hundredth anniversary of the apparition of Our Blessed Mother to Sister (now Saint) Catherine Labouré. Mary revealed the design of the Miraculous Medal to Catherine, a novice of the Daughters of Charity, at rue du Bac in Paris on November 27, 1830.

PRAYER TO OUR LADY OF THE MIRACULOUS MEDAL

O Immaculate Virgin Mary, Mother of our Lord Jesus and our Mother, penetrated with the most lively confidence in your all-powerful and never-failing intercession, manifested so often through the Miraculous Medal, we your loving and trustful children implore you to obtain for us the graces and favors we ask during this novena, if they be beneficial to our immortal souls and the souls for whom we pray. (Here privately form your petitions.) You know, O Mary, how often our souls have been the sanctuaries of your Son who hates iniquity. Obtain for us then a deep hatred of sin and that purity of heart which will attach us to God alone so that our every thought, word, and deed may tend to his greater glory. Obtain for us also a spirit of prayer and self-denial that we may recover by penance what we have lost by sin and at length attain to that blessed abode where you are the queen of angels and of men. Amen.

ABOUT THE SHRINE

World travelers say that Mary's Central Shrine is among the most beautiful of all the Marian shrines that jewel this earth. The glow of hundreds of votive lamps plays over the marble of its sea-green columns and wine-red bays, and glows in the warm gold and rich colors of its brilliant mosaics. Above the tabernacle of the magnificent altar, bathed in white radiance, stands the exquisite Carrara-marble statue of Our Lady of the Miraculous Medal, with arms outstretched as if to embrace all who kneel in petition before her. This statue has been acclaimed as one of the most beautiful representations of Our Lady in the world.

Such is the throne room of the Immaculate Queen of Heaven, where eager hearts leap up to her loving embrace—and where, by the unaccountable blessings and favors she showers on those who have recourse to her, she proves she is indeed the powerful Mother of God!

Another smaller shrine is located on the ground floor of the chapel, directly below Mary's Central Shrine. In this lower shrine, the statue above the altar represents Our Lady as she appeared at the start of the second apparition to Saint Catherine Labouré, during which Mary manifested the design of the Miraculous Medal.

SHRINE INFORMATION

Central Shrine of Our Lady of the Miraculous Medal
500 East Chelten Avenue
Philadelphia, PA 19144
(800) 523-3674
(215) 848-1010
fax: (215) 848-1014

TOURIST INFORMATION

No hotel accommodations are located in the immediate area. Specific information can be obtained by contacting

Tourist Information and Visitor's Bureau
1515 Market Street
Philadelphia, PA 19102
(215) 636-1666

DIRECTIONS TO THE SHRINE

Central Shrine of Our Lady of the Miraculous Medal is located in northern Philadelphia. The best way to travel to the shrine is by private car or tourist bus.

FROM NEW YORK, NORTHERN NEW JERSEY, AND WESTERN POINTS

Via the Pennsylvania Turnpike (I-76/I-276): Leave the turnpike at the Fort Washington Interchange; * drive south on Rte. 309 Freeway to its connection with Ogontz Avenue, and continue south on Ogontz Avenue to Wyncote Avenue (6800). Turn right on Wyncote (which runs diagonally from Ogontz) and continue until Wyncote joins Chelten Avenue, then go straight ahead on Chelten to the shrine.

FROM SCRANTON, ALLENTOWN, AND BETHLEHEM AREAS

Take the Northeast Extension of the Pennsylvania Turnpike (Rte. 9) to the end; go left (east) on the turnpike (I-276) to the Fort Washington Interchange, then follow the directions at * just above.

FROM EASTON AND POCONO REGION

Take Rte. 611 via Easton Road to Willow Grove, where it meets Old York Road. Go south on Old York Road (which enters Philadelphia at 7200) to Chelten Avenue (6400). Go right on Chelten Avenue to the shrine. (The alternate route is by the Northeast Extension, as above.)

FROM SOUTHERN NEW JERSEY AND SOUTHERN POINTS

Take the Schuylkill Expressway (I-76) north to the City Avenue Interchange (watch for the directional sign reading, "City Ave. Bridge—Germantown—Keep Right"). Cross City Avenue Bridge over the

Schuylkill River to Ridge Avenue. Go right on Ridge Avenue to Midvale Avenue; go left on Midvale to Wissahickon Avenue; go left on Wissahickon to Chelten Avenue (the second traffic light); go right on Chelten Avenue to the shrine.

FOR FIRST-TIME PILGRIMS

The Central Shrine of Our Lady of the Miraculous Medal was built in 1927 and is under the care of the Vincentian Community (the Congregation of the Mission) of the Eastern Province of the United States. The shrine is open year-round on Tuesday through Sunday from 11:00 A.M. to 4:00 P.M. and on Mondays all day. Mass is celebrated on Mondays at 7:00 and 9:00 A.M. and 12:05 P.M.; Tuesday through Saturday at 8:00 A.M. and 12:05 P.M.; and on Sundays and holy days at 9:00 A.M.

Miraculous Medal novena services are scheduled each Monday at 7:00 and 9:00 A.M. with Mass, and every hour from 2:00 through 8:00 P.M. with Benediction (no Mass). Confessions are heard before each novena service.

There is an elevator from street level to the shrine. Off-street parking is available. Pilgrims may also wish to visit the gift shop.

OF SPECIAL INTEREST

Unlike Lourdes and other famous shrines, the Central Shrine of Our Lady of the Miraculous Medal has no stacks of crutches or braces or canes left after miraculous cures. While physical cures have been reported, the history of this shrine reflects the miracles of graces worked in the secrecy of the confessional. Countless numbers have told how they have experienced God's mercy and healing through the sacrament of reconciliation.

+‖+
+‖+

The Lady Chapel

ST. PATRICK'S CATHEDRAL
NEW YORK, NEW YORK

St. Patrick's Cathedral was the dream of John Hughes, the first archbishop of New York. James Renwick, the noted mid-nineteenth-century architect, crystallized that dream in blueprints of a great Gothic cathedral. Three years after the foundation had been laid, tragedy struck this nation—the horror of the Civil War. Weeds grew wild over what should have been a testimony to humanity's love, and not until fourteen years after the end of the Civil War was the cathedral opened, completed under the direction of John Cardinal McCloskey. However, it was not in its present completed form. The spires were not lifted until about ten years later, and the Lady Chapel was added at the turn of the century, but it was true to the traditional Gothic style common in European churches built from the thirteenth to the fifteenth centuries.

PRAYER TO OUR LADY OF THE BLESSED SACRAMENT

O Virgin Mary, Our Lady of the Blessed Sacrament, thou glory of the Christian people, joy of the universal Church, salvation of the whole world, pray for us, and awaken in all believers a lively devotion toward the most holy Eucharist, so that we may be made worthy to receive that same Eucharist each day. Amen.

ABOUT THE SHRINE

The architect had included in his original design a small chapel behind the main altar, in keeping with the traditional plan of the great Gothic cathedrals of England and continental Europe. In the Middle Ages, this chapel was dedicated to the Virgin Mary and came to be known as the Chapel of Our Lady, or more simply as the Lady Chapel. However, Renwick's plan was modified, and St. Patrick's, at its completion, terminated abruptly a few feet behind the apsidal columns. A Lady Chapel was established at the east end of the north aisle.

In 1900 plans were made for the new Lady Chapel. Fourteen architects from America, England, and France took part in the competition to remodel the flat east end of the cathedral and to design a Lady Chapel. Charles T. Mathews's design was chosen, and construction began in 1901. The cathedral was lengthened, and by continuing the side aisles behind the main altar, a graceful vista was opened up running the length of the nave, through the sanctuary, and into the chapel. The design is patterned on the thirteenth-century French Gothic style, more ornate and elaborate than that of the rest of the cathedral.

The Lady Chapel is built of Vermont marble with stone interior and pavement of polished Sienna marble inlaid in a Gothic pattern. Fifteen stained-glass windows, installed between 1912 and 1934, were designed by Paul Woodroffe in the manner of the medallion windows in the cathedral at Chartres, France.

The first Mass in the Lady Chapel was celebrated at Christmas, 1906.

SHRINE INFORMATION

St. Patrick's Cathedral Parish House
460 Madison Avenue
New York, NY 10022
(212) 753-2261

DIRECTIONS TO THE SHRINE

St. Patrick's Cathedral is located between Madison Avenue and Fifth Avenue, just blocks south of Central Park and adjacent to Rockefeller Center. The cathedral occupies the city block that is bordered on the north by East 51st Street and on the southern exposure by East 50th Street. It may well be one of the most well-known addresses in the Catholic world. It is easily accessible by foot or by taxi. First-time visitors are advised not to drive your own car because parking in Manhattan is very expensive and difficult to find.

FOR FIRST–TIME PILGRIMS

To enter St. Patrick's Cathedral for the first time is a wonderful experience that has a certain "specialness" about it. You enter the cathedral from one of the world's busiest and most secular urban cities and find yourself in a space that is calm and sacred, in stark contrast to the city outside. A first-time pilgrim is advised to enter the cathedral and to resist the desire to begin immediately exploring. It is much better to walk down the central aisle, choose a seat, spend a few moments in prayer, and then begin to familiarize yourself with your surroundings.

✝╫✝
✝╫✝

Lourdes in Litchfield

MONTFORT MISSIONARIES
LITCHFIELD, CONNECTICUT

"Pray to God for sinners."
"Penance, penance, penance."
WORDS OF OUR LADY OF LOURDES

The Grotto of Our Lady of Lourdes in France has been known throughout the world for more than a century. It was there that the

The Grotto of Our Lady at Lourdes in Litchfield commemorates the appearance of Our Lady of Lourdes to Saint Bernadette.
(Anthony F. Chiffolo)

Mother of God appeared in 1858 to a simple country child. She spoke to Bernadette Soubirous and, through her, to all of us. As Bernadette listened, she heard words of hope and reconciliation, words that could find fulfillment only if they were taken to heart. In 1954, which was proclaimed a "Marian Year" by Pope Pius XII, the Montfort Missionaries, a religious community of priests and brothers, undertook a project to contribute to the fulfillment of Our Lady's wishes, setting about to make Our Lady's message at Lourdes come alive in the New England area.

ABOUT THE SHRINE

The principle shrine at Lourdes in Litchfield is the Grotto of Our Lady. It is constructed of local fieldstone in a natural rock hedge and modeled after the actual grotto in Lourdes, France. In addition to several other shrines, the thirty-five acres of shrine grounds also include a winding and ascending Way of the Cross, which culminates in the crucifixion scene that dominates the entire shrine area and valley below.

SHRINE INFORMATION

Reverend Father Director
Lourdes in Litchfield
P.O. Box 667
Litchfield, CT 06759-0667
(860) 567-1041

TOURIST INFORMATION

Contact the Reverend Father Director at Lourdes in Litchfield for specific information regarding hotels and eating establishments. Adjacent to the parking lot is a picnic area with tables and fireplaces for the convenience of pilgrims and visitors. In addition, facilities for catered meals are available upon prior arrangements with the shrine director. Ample parking for cars and buses is available, for individual and group pilgrimages. Persons with disabilities may park closer to the grotto by following the appropriate signs.

DIRECTIONS TO THE SHRINE

Lourdes in Litchfield is located about fifteen miles north-northwest of Waterbury, Connecticut.

FROM NEW YORK CITY, LONG ISLAND, NEW JERSEY

Take the New England Thruway (I-95) north to exit 21N. Go three miles west on I-287, then north onto I-684 toward Brewster. After twenty-seven miles, at exit 9E, take I-84 east, for thirty-seven miles. At exit 20, turn left onto Rte. 8 north, make a quick merge right, and get off at exit 38. * Go left onto Rte. 254, which makes a sharp left after one mile. Travel seven miles to the end. Turn left on Rte. 118; the shrine entrance is a quarter mile down the hill on the right.

Or, from the Connecticut Turnpike (I-95) north to Bridgeport: at exit 27A, take Rte. 8 north to exit 38, then follow the directions at * just above.

Or, from the Bridgeport Ferry: go right at the fifth light, jog left and right onto Rte. 8 north. Take exit 38, then follow the directions at * above.

FROM HARTFORD

Take I-84 westbound to exit 39. Take Rte. 4 westbound through Unionville to Harwinton. In Harwinton take Rte. 118 westbound to Litchfield. The shrine entrance is on Rte. 118 before you enter the center of town.

FROM BOSTON

Take the Massachusetts Turnpike (I-90) westbound to exit 9. Take I-84 southbound through Hartford. Follow the Hartford directions.

FROM ALBANY

Take the New York Thruway (I-90) eastbound to the Massachusetts Turnpike (I-90). Turn off at exit 2 (Rte. 20). Take Rte. 20 eastbound to Rte. 8. Take Rte. 8 southbound to exit 42 (Rte. 118) and turn right. Take Rte. 118 westbound for five miles. The shrine entrance is on Rte. 118 before you enter the center of town.

FROM PROVIDENCE

Take Rte. 44 or Rte. 6 westbound to I-384/I-84 through Hartford. Follow the Hartford directions.

FROM SPRINGFIELD, MASSACHUSETTS

Take I-91 southbound to Hartford. Take I-84 westbound through Hartford. Follow the Hartford directions.

FOR FIRST-TIME PILGRIMS

Public devotions and services are held from the first Sunday in May to mid-October. The shrine grounds are open to the public year-round. Activities can take place daily at the shrine and are not affected by inclement weather. Mass can be offered in the Pilgrim Hall in place of the grotto. Daily Mass is celebrated at 11:30 A.M. except on Mondays.

Mass on Sunday in celebrated at 11:30 A.M. in the grotto; at 1:45 P.M. is the Stations of the Cross; and at 3:00 P.M. are the Benediction and rosary.

OF SPECIAL INTEREST

Lourdes in Litchfield has been constructed to foster devotion to Jesus through an understanding of Mary as the perfect Christian, or first pilgrim, to the heavenly Jerusalem. Through devotion to Mary at this shrine, and especially in the liturgical celebration of the Eucharist, the Montfort Missionaries are making an effort to outwardly express for the people of God their pilgrimage to full life in Jesus Christ.

"In her maternal love may Mary lead you to her Son!"

$$+ \| + \atop + \| +$$

Madonna, Queen of the Universe National Shrine

DON ORIONE FATHERS
BOSTON, MASSACHUSETTS

On December 8, 1943, Arrigo Minerbi, a renowned Italian-Jewish sculptor fleeing from the Nazis, was given refuge in the houses of the Don Orione Fathers in Rome, where he remained until the war ended. As a personal act of thanksgiving on his part and to fulfill a vow made by the people of Rome to the Blessed Mother, Minerbi agreed to create a statue of Mary.

When the friends and benefactors of the nascent works of charity of Don Orione in the States saw the completed statue in Rome, they asked Minerbi to make another one for Boston. In this way they sought to fulfill the desire of Don Orione himself that beside every work of charity (in this particular case the nursing home for the elderly) there would be a work of faith. Richard Cardinal Cushing of Boston gave his full approval for the erection of a shrine to Our Blessed Lady and suggested the title "Queen of the Universe," in keeping with the recently proclaimed dogma of the Assumption of Mary.

HAIL MARY

Hail Mary, full of grace, the Lord is with thee. Blessed art thou among women, and blessed is the fruit of thy womb, Jesus. Holy Mary, Mother of God, pray for us sinners, now and at the hour of our death. Amen.

ABOUT THE SHRINE

The Madonna, Queen of the Universe National Shrine was founded in 1954 and is cared for by the Don Orione Fathers, a religious congregation of Italian origin. The thirty-five-foot statue of the Blessed Mother venerated here is an exact copy of the one that stands on top of Monte Mario in Rome. Both statues were created by the sculptor Arrigo Minerbi.

SHRINE INFORMATION

Madonna, Queen of the Universe National Shrine
111 Orient Avenue
East Boston, MA 02128
(617) 569-2100

TOURIST INFORMATION

Specific information regarding restaurant and hotel accommodations can be obtained from the above address. Large pilgrim groups with prior reservations may have a reasonably priced meal at the shrine.

DIRECTIONS TO THE SHRINE

The shrine, located in East Boston, is close to Logan International Airport, just north of central Boston. It is accessible on the Blue Line of the MBTA, Suffolk Downs Station, and can be easily reached by car: Go north on Hwy. 1 to Boardmen Street, east on Boardmen for a very short distance to Palermo, again a very short distance and continue east to your first left, proceeding north. You will cross Gladstone Street, and the next street will be Orient Avenue. Turn right on Orient and the shrine will be straight ahead.

For First-Time Pilgrims

The Madonna, Queen of the Universe National Shrine is open year-round and is wheelchair accessible. A large Pilgrim Reception Center and a gift shop are available to all pilgrims. Mass is celebrated on the weekdays at 8:30 A.M. and 7:30 P.M. and on Sunday at 11:00 A.M. and 4:30 P.M. Special Masses for groups may be arranged with the shrine. Confessions are heard before all Masses and on Saturdays from 6:30–7:20 P.M. Pilgrims may attend the recitation of the holy rosary during the week at 7:00 P.M. and on Sunday at 3:30 P.M. and Benediction on Sunday at 3:45 P.M.

Of Special Interest

Visitors to the Madonna Shrine might enjoy a side trip to Logan International Airport, a short distance away. Inside the airport is Our Lady of the Airways Chapel, inspired by Richard Cardinal Cushing in 1952. It is used for daily Mass and devotional visits every day of the week. Inscribed on the pillar of the altar is the prayer that is still prayed by people all over the world: "We fly to your patronage, O Holy Mother of God; despise not our petitions in our necessity but deliver us always from all dangers, O glorious and Blessed Virgin."

Marian Shrine
SALESIANS OF DON BOSCO
WEST HAVERSTRAW, NEW YORK

Spread devotion to Mary, Help of Christians, and you will see miracles.
SAINT JOHN BOSCO

According to the story that is often repeated, while asleep in his little room, John Bosco was confronted by a menacing crowd of unruly youths, all cursing and fighting. He bravely took them on with his bare fists, but soon realized he was no match for them. Providentially, a "majestic" man reached out to him, pulled him out of the fray, and then promptly ordered him to go back into that crowd and take charge, this time "not with blows but with kindness." John protested: "Why do

you ask impossible things of me? Who are you, anyway?" "Ask my Mother," was the reply. "I will give her as your teacher and guide, and she will make it all possible." At that moment a beautiful Lady stood by John, patted him gently on the head, and, taking him by the hand, reassured him: "In due time you will understand."

As his dream became a reality, John Bosco experienced the wonderful help and guidance of his Lady at every crucial step in his life. So grateful was he that he erected a Shrine Church in Turin, Italy, under the title of "Mary, Help of Christians." His Salesians

The bronze rosary Madonna statue at the Marian Shrine is located in a lovely woodland setting on the west bank of the Hudson River. *(Anthony F. Chiffolo)*

carried the "new" devotion to Mary to the four corners of the globe, erecting hundreds of shrines to Don Bosco's Madonna. The Marian Shrine here came into being by the same charism.

PRAYER TO MARY, HELP OF CHRISTIANS

Most Holy and Immaculate Virgin Mary, our tender Mother and mighty help of Christians, we dedicate ourselves completely to your dear love and holy service. We dedicate to you our minds and our thoughts, our hearts and all our affections, our bodies and our senses and all our strength; we promise to be ever willing to labor for the greater glory of God and the salvation of souls. Grant to us, O Mary, Help of Christians, to be gathered under your maternal protection. May the thought of the love you bear toward your devoted sons and daughters be a great source of strength for us and make us victors over the enemies of our salvation, both in life and in death, so that we may come to stand with you in the beauty of paradise. Amen.

About the Shrine

The Salesians of Don Bosco built a rosary way in West Haverstraw in 1954 in observance of the Marian Year. Fifteen life-size marble statues were placed along a wooded path. People came in increasing numbers to pray along this gospel trail. As the number of pilgrims grew, the shrine was formally established.

Over the years, additional items were added to beautify the Marian shrine. These include a forty-eight-foot bronze rosary Madonna statue; the majestic altar of Mary that serves as an outdoor cathedral; a glass-enclosed pavilion chapel; grottoes depicting the apparitions at Fátima and Lourdes; the Becchi House (a replica of the house where Saint John Bosco grew up); the large, marble Stations of the Cross; and a memorial to the unborn.

Shrine Information

Marian Shrine
Filors Lane
P.O. Box 9000
West Haverstraw, NY 10993-9000
(914) 947-2200
fax: (914) 947-2203
e-mail: mhcshrine@aol.com

Tourist Information

The shrine has available for pilgrims a snack bar, a cafeteria, and picnic groves. Unfortunately, there are no convents, monasteries, or pilgrim housing in the area. There are some commercial motels about twenty minutes from the shrine, including

- The Bear Mountain Inn, an historic, rustic inn located on extensive acreage:
  Rte. 9W
  Harriman State Park, New York
  (914) 786-2731
- The Hotel Thayer, located on the grounds of the U.S. Military Academy
  Thayer Road
  West Point, New York

There are several motels in the adjacent town of Highland Falls, New York. Specific information regarding restaurants and hotel accommodations can be obtained by contacting the local tourist office:

Rockland County Tourism
11 New Hempstead Road
New City, NY 10956
(914) 638-5800
fax: (914) 353-6244

DIRECTIONS TO THE SHRINE

The easiest way to the shrine is by car. The Palisades Interstate Parkway runs north and south. Exit 14 is one and a half miles from the shrine entrance. A second choice would be by bus or car to Stony Point, New York. Pick up 9W and the Palisades Parkway off the three bridges: George Washington, Tappan Zee, or Bear Mountain. The shrine is just twenty-nine miles north of the George Washington Bridge, which crosses from northern Manhattan to New Jersey.

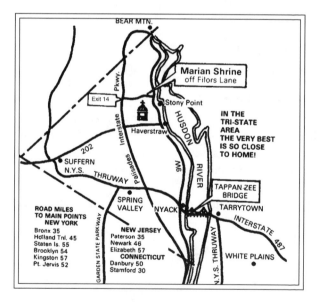

FOR FIRST-TIME PILGRIMS

The Marian Shrine is located in a lovely woodland setting on the west bank of the Hudson River, halfway between the George Washington Bridge and West Point. The picturesque retreat site on two hundred acres of breathtaking scenery makes an ideal spot for prayer pilgrimages and picnics and offers a spectacular view of the river at its widest and most historic point. Just to the north is "Mad" Anthony Wayne country, Stony Point, where his American forces launched a successful attack on the British to secure fortifications and return control of the river to the Continental Army. Historic markers depict the various scenes and sequences of the battle.

The shrine is a place for spiritual renewal through pilgrimages, retreats, and days of study and recollection. The Salesians strive to make the shrine a place where all can encounter the Lord with the help of Mary. The Blessed Sacrament Chapel is open for prayer and meditation Sundays from 9:00 A.M. to 5:00 P.M. Masses are celebrated daily at noon and on Sundays at 11:00 A.M. and 12:30 P.M. May to October and noon November to April. Confessions can be heard before each Mass or upon request. The rosary is said after daily Mass, and Eucharistic adoration is Wednesdays at 8:00 P.M.

Facilities include the Adult Retreat Center, Youth Retreat Center, Renewal Center (ample space for workshops), overnight accommodations (for groups only), the religious bookstore, and the gift shop.

OF SPECIAL INTEREST

Saint John Bosco's statue greets pilgrims when they first arrive for prayer at the Pavilion Chapel. A short distance beyond is a faithful replica of his birthplace, just as it is at Becchi, Italy. This unusual, "unfinished" structure serves as a unique reminder of "our roots," of Saint John Bosco's poverty and hard work, as well as his first "dream," or vision, which was granted him here concerning his future mission for youth.

+‖+
+‖+

National Blue Army Shrine of the Immaculate Heart of Mary

WASHINGTON, NEW JERSEY

In certain places the Mother's presence is felt in a particularly vivid way.
These places sometimes radiate their light over a great distance and draw
people from afar. Their radiance may extend over a diocese,
a whole nation or, at times, over several countries and even continents.
These places are the Marian sanctuaries or shrines.

POPE JOHN PAUL II, MAY 13, 1982, FÁTIMA

Mary, the Mother of God, appeared to three shepherd children at Fátima, Portugal, in 1917. Through a series of six apparitions from May 13 through October 13, the Blessed Virgin Mary invited all humankind to prayer, conversion, consecration, and reparation as the sure means of obtaining world peace. Her message was validated by the Miracle of the Sun on October 13, 1917. More than seventy thousand persons, including atheists, within a thirty-mile radius of Fátima saw the sun make abrupt movements in the sky and plunge toward the

The National Blue Army Shrine of the Immaculate Heart of Mary encourages pilgrims to learn and live Our Lady of Fátima's vital message of prayer, conversion, reparation, and consecration for world peace. *(National Blue Army Shrine of the Immaculate Heart of Mary)*

earth. Our Lady of Fátima prophesied the rise of communism, World War II, and persecution for the Church, but added that in the end her Immaculate Heart would triumph and an era of peace would be granted to humankind.

The National Blue Army Shrine of the Immaculate Heart of Mary, completed in 1978, offers pilgrims a peaceful setting for prayer and meditation. The shrine is dedicated to the Immaculate Heart of Mary in line with the Fátima message and encourages pilgrims to learn and live this vital message of prayer, conversion, reparation, and consecration that can bring world peace.

ABOUT THE SHRINE

The Blue Army of Our Lady of Fátima completed the Shrine of the Immaculate Heart of Mary in 1978 as a center of Eucharistic and Marian devotion. It is particularly dedicated to the Immaculate Heart of Mary and the Fátima message. The roof of the shrine represents Mary's mantle flowing over and protecting her children. The crown reminds us that Mary is not only a mother, but our queen, the Queen of Heaven. The special charism of the shrine is peace, and pilgrims who come with faith, love, and devotion to honor the Eucharistic Heart of Jesus and the Immaculate Heart of his Mother will experience a unique closeness to Jesus and Mary.

SHRINE INFORMATION

Pilgrimage Coordinator
Shrine of the Immaculate Heart of Mary
Box 976
Washington, NJ 07885-0976
(908) 689-1700 ext. 30
fax: (908) 689-MARY
e-mail: bluearmy@ix.netcom.com
website: http://www.bluearmy.com

TOURIST INFORMATION

There are three Washingtons in New Jersey. The Shrine of the Immaculate Heart of Mary is located in rural northwestern New Jersey in Washington Township, Warren County, ten minutes from the town of Washington, New Jersey, and about fifteen miles east of Easton, Pennsylvania. There are no facilities for lodging at the shrine; therefore, pilgrims must make their own reservations at nearby motels in advance. Some suggested lodgings:

- Holiday Inn-Phillipsburg: 1324 Rte. 22 East (Jct. I-78), Phillipsburg, NJ 08865, (908) 454-9771
- Holiday Inn-Clinton: Rte. 173, Clinton, NJ 08809, (908) 735-5111
- Phillipsburg Inn: 1315 Hwy. 22 West (Jct. I-78), Phillipsburg, NJ 08865, (908) 454-6461 or (800) 555-5952
- Broadway Motel: State Hwy. 57 West, Washington, NJ 07882, (908) 689-3366
- Ralph's Motel: Rte. 57 West, Port Murray, NJ 07865, (908) 689-5335
- Best Western Easton Inn: 185 South 3rd St., Easton, PA 18042, (800) 882-0113 or (610) 253-9131
- Days Inn: Rte. 22 West 25th Street Exit, Easton, PA 18042, (800) 329-7466 or (610) 253-0546

A food vendor is available on the thirteenth of each month from May through October, and on other major days. No facilities for eating indoors are available; however, picnic areas are provided (no grills or fires are permitted). There is a wide variety of restaurants in the nearby area.

DIRECTIONS TO THE SHRINE

National Blue Army Shrine of the Immaculate Heart of Mary is located about fifty-five miles west of New York City, thirty-five miles north of Trenton, and fifteen miles northeast of Easton, Pennsylvania. There is no direct public transportation to the shrine. All buses must park in the lower parking lot. Limited parking is available at the Holy House for short intervals, except during major events, when no parking is allowed.

FROM GEORGE WASHINGTON BRIDGE, NEW YORK CITY/ NEW ENGLAND

Take I-80 west to Allamuchy (exit 19). At the exit make a left onto Rte. 517 south through Hackettstown (it will merge with Rte. 182). Go right on Rte. 57 west to Washington. See local area directions below.

FROM STATEN ISLAND, LONG ISLAND, BROOKLYN, QUEENS, ETC.

Take the Verrazano Narrows Bridge to the Staten Island Expressway, to Outerbridge Crossing (Rte. 440), I-287 north to I-78 west to Rte. 31 north (exit 17) to Washington.

FROM NEWARK, JERSEY CITY AREA, SOMERVILLE AREA

Take I-78 west to Rte. 31 north (exit 17) to Washington.

FROM PHILADELPHIA

Take I-95 north to exit 4B (Pennington exit) to Rte. 31 north to Washington.

FROM TRENTON AND FLEMINTON

Take Rte. 31 north to Washington.

FROM LEHIGH VALLEY INTERNATIONAL AIRPORT

Take Rte. 22 east to Rte. 57 east to Rte. 31 south in Washington.

FROM MIDWEST STATES, PENNSYLVANIA, OHIO, MICHIGAN, ETC.

Take I-80 east to the Delaware Water Gap area, to Rte. 46 east to Rte. 31 south to Washington.

LOCAL AREA DIRECTIONS

At the traffic light intersection of Rtes. 57 and 31, take Rte. 31 south for two miles. Watch for signs "Blue Army Shrine" and "Asbury." Make a right onto Asbury Road (Rte. 632 west). Continue as below at *.

When traveling on Rte. 31 north: Soon after passing the sign for Hampton, Asbury, and Blue Army Shrine, at the traffic light turn left onto Asbury Road (Rte. 632 west). Continue as below at *.

*Drive for one mile. Watch for another Blue Army sign. Turn right onto Cemetery Hill Road. Proceed another mile and turn left at the "Blue Army Shrine" sign (Mountain View Road). Continue a quarter mile to the shrine.

FOR FIRST-TIME PILGRIMS

Except for the thirteenth of each month from May to October, the shrine is open daily for the celebration of Mass, confession, and the rosary. The shrine is served by the Oblates of the Virgin Mary, the Handmaids of Mary Immaculate, and a corps of dedicated volunteers. Their mission is to assist the pilgrim in achieving a spiritually enriching visit to the shrine. A bus coordinator is vital to the success of group pilgrimages, and the group leader should submit a completed pilgrimage reservation form (at least two weeks in advance) for each group (ten or more) visiting the shrine.

No smoking and no pets are permitted on the shrine grounds.

Please note: The dress code is strictly enforced at the Shrine of the Immaculate Heart of Mary. Persons not dressed according to the code as listed below may not remain on the premises:

- no shorts (men, women)
- no sundresses or mini-skirts
- no halters or revealing attire
- shirt and shoes required

To avoid any embarrassment, leaders of pilgrimages are asked to inform their group about the dress code prior to their coming to the shrine. Leaders should also check to see that this code is honored.

OF SPECIAL INTEREST

At Fátima, Our Lady predicted the moral and spiritual breakdown of our society if her requests were not heeded. She offered us a spiritual means for restoring the moral order and establishing peace in the world. Her message is a message of hope and of sure guidance in this era of moral confusion. Our Lady promised that in the end her Immaculate Heart will triumph and an era of peace will be granted to humankind.

The dramatic prophecies were made to the children immediately after they were shown a vision of hell on July 13, 1917. The vision of hell is the first part of what has been called the Fátima Secret. The second part is a request for devotion to the Immaculate Heart of Mary. The third part of the secret, the subject of widespread speculation, has not yet been made public by the Holy Father.

National Shrine of the Divine Mercy

ASSOCIATION OF MARIAN HELPERS
STOCKBRIDGE, MASSACHUSETTS

The National Shrine of the Divine Mercy is not a Marian shrine but rather has been erected to house the sacred image of Our Lord as "The Divine Mercy." This sacred and popular image, which had become the object of spontaneous pilgrimages since it was first enshrined in the tiny Eden Hill Chapel in 1945, is nevertheless a shrine that is "close to the heart of our Blessed Mother," and it is thus appropriately included here. The "Chaplet to Divine Mercy" that is daily prayed at the shrine is prayed using ordinary rosary beads of five decades, which serves as a constant reminder of the connection between our Blessed Mother and her merciful Son.

Every day at three in the afternoon the chapel bell invites the faithful who come to Eden Hill to pray to Our Lord as "The Divine Mercy." *(Anthony F. Chiffolo)*

The shrine was inspired by faithful pilgrims from all over the country who had experienced the wonderful effects of the "Message of the Divine Mercy," revealed through Blessed Faustina Kowalska, as well as of the devotion associated with it. It was also funded by their freewill offerings as a grateful tribute to the tender mercy they had experienced God pouring out upon them.

PRAYER FOR INTERCESSION

Let intercession be made for us, we beseech thee, O Lord Jesus Christ, now and at the hour of our death, before the throne of thy Mercy, by the blessed Virgin Mary, thy Mother, whose most holy soul was pierced by a sword of sorrow in the hour of thy bitter passion. Through thee, Jesus Christ, Savior of the World, who with the Father and the Holy Spirit lives and reigns, world without end. Amen.

ABOUT THE SHRINE

Every day at three in the afternoon, "The Hour of Great Mercy," the chapel bell invites the faithful who come to Eden Hill to implore God's mercy for themselves and the world, especially for sinners, both by calling to mind Christ's abandonment at the moment of his agony and his love for us—expressed by the gushing of the Blood and Water from his Heart as a transfusion into us of his divine life when his side was pierced by a lance—and by offering appropriate prayers. The "Chaplet to the Divine Mercy," one of the forms of devotion to the Divine Mercy revealed through Blessed Faustina, is also recited at this time.

The relic of Blessed Faustina is now enshrined in a side altar at the shrine. A specially commissioned wood carving was blessed by Bernard Cardinal Law, archbishop of Boston, in 1993. The shrine was constructed entirely by hand by local stonemasons and woodcarvers using locally found materials.

SHRINE INFORMATION

Shrine of the Divine Mercy
Eden Hill
Stockbridge, MA 01262
(413) 298-1119
e-mail: dmshrine@aol.com

TOURIST INFORMATION

The spiritual home of the Association of Marian Helpers, National Shrine of the Divine Mercy is located on Eden Hill in Stockbridge, Massachusetts, close to the site of the first Christian missions to the native people of the Berkshires. It adjoins Eden Hall, the former Field's family "summer cottage" and later the Saint Edmund's Episcopal School for boys, now the Headquarters of the St. Stanislaus Kostka Province of the Marians of the Immaculate Conception.

Specific information regarding restaurant and hotel accommodations can be obtained by writing or calling the shrine at the above address.

DIRECTIONS TO THE SHRINE

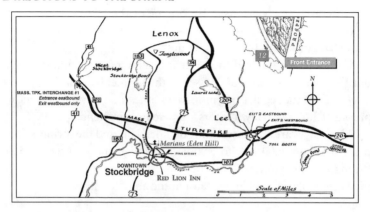

National Shrine of the Divine Mercy, in Stockbridge, Massachusetts, is located about ten miles south of Pittsfield.

FROM PENNSYLVANIA, NEW YORK, OR NEW JERSEY

Take the New York Thruway (I-87) north to exit 21A, the exit at the intersection of I-90 (the Berkshire section of the Thruway), and proceed east. Exit at B3 (Austerlitz) and follow the signs to Rte. 22 south (less than a mile), then to Rte. 102 east, through West Stockbridge and into Stockbridge.

FROM NORTH OF THE MASSACHUSETTS TURNPIKE

Take Rte. 7 south and follow the signs to Stockbridge.

FROM SOUTH OF THE MASSACHUSETTS TURNPIKE

Take Rte. 7 north from Connecticut.

FROM THE EAST VIA THE MASSACHUSETTS TURNPIKE

Take I-90 west to exit 2 (Lee) and follow Rte. 102 to Stockbridge.

FOR FIRST-TIME PILGRIMS

Visitors are always welcomed to attend Mass at the National Shrine of the Divine Mercy at 7:15 A.M. on weekdays; at 8:00 A.M. on Saturdays, holy days, and holidays; and at 10:30 A.M. on Sundays. The "Chaplet to the Divine Mercy" is prayed daily at the National Shrine of the Divine Mercy at 3:00 P.M. On Sundays, the chaplet is celebrated with Benediction. The Marians at the Shrine of the Divine Mercy daily remember, in prayer and holy Mass, all Marian Associates and those who write or call with prayer requests.

Marian Associates and their intentions are remembered throughout the year in novenas of Masses at the shrine. Novena Masses are celebrated at the regular morning Mass times, and novena prayers are prayed at 3:00 P.M. daily. Visitors are welcome to attend.

Pilgrimages are always welcome on Eden Hill, and the shrine is open every day from 6:00 A.M. to 6:00 P.M. Bus pilgrimages are organized throughout the year. All bus groups must prearrange their visit with the Shrine Pilgrimage Coordinator at the above address.

OF SPECIAL INTEREST

The word *novena* comes from the Latin meaning "nine each." It is a prayer or holy Mass that is offered for nine consecutive days. Scripturally, novenas get their origin from the nine days of prayer before Pentecost. The apostles and disciples, in obedience to the Lord, gathered in the upper room and devoted themselves to constant prayer, together with Mary, the Mother of Jesus. Jesus exhorted us to continually ask, seek, and knock for what we need, and his parables give strong examples of the value of persistence in prayer. We should consider novenas as persistent, persevering prayer for special needs and preparation for solemn feasts.

National Shrine of Our Lady of Guadalupe

IMMACULATE CONCEPTION CHURCH
ALLENTOWN, PENNSYLVANIA

On a cold December morning many years ago, a poor man named Juan Diego was hurrying to Mass for the feast of the Immaculate Conception. Juan was stopped by beautiful music not of this world and favored with a vision whose splendor rivaled the brilliance of the sun in the central Mexican highlands. That was the beginning of the visit of Our Lady of Guadalupe to Mexico, to the Americas, a visit that culminated in granting to these lands a most singular blessing. On December 12, 1531, a portrait of the Mother of God appeared miraculously on the poor cactus-fiber cloak, the *tilma*, of the seer. More than four centuries later, the *tilma* has not deteriorated, and the sacred image has not faded. Still today, pilgrims can go, as did our Holy Father "Juan Pablo II" in his first pilgrimage as pope, to Mexico and encounter the Blessed Mother, as she looked when she stood before the humble Juan Diego at the beginning of Christendom in the New World.

PRAYER TO OUR LADY OF GUADALUPE

Beautiful Lady of Tepeyac Hill, clothed in rays of sunshine bright, softly etched on a peasant's cloak, your radiant beauty brings delight. Not to the Fathers did you appear, nor to bishops in hallowed hall. To a people oppressed, you turn your face; to a race despised, you call. From these people you chose a son, Juan Diego, suffering servant; Juan Diego, simple Aztec saint. As roses blossomed in rocky soil, out of season, out of place, so did hearts frozen in hatred melt, and so did radiant faith take root. Virgin Mother of our God, soften our hearts and fill them now; call us out of our narrowness; challenge us in our shallowness, and bring us into your Son's embrace. Amen.

ABOUT THE SHRINE

In 1974 Immaculate Conception Church in Allentown, Pennsylvania, was chosen to house the U.S. National Shrine of Our Lady of Guadalupe, Mother of the Americas. A special committee of the U.S. Catholic Conference had decided to establish a national shrine in this country because Our Lady of Guadalupe is Mother of all the Americas, including the United States, where Our Lady was already honored as patroness under her title "The Immaculate Conception." An image of Our Lady of Guadalupe was produced for the shrine in the exact dimensions of the original miraculous image in Mexico City, resembling the original in color and in every detail more closely than any other reproduction. This amazing likeness has given rise to the saying "If you can't go to Mexico, go to Allentown."

SHRINE INFORMATION

National Shrine of Our Lady of Guadalupe
Immaculate Conception Church
501 Ridge Avenue
Allentown, PA 18102
(610) 820-5255

TOURIST INFORMATION

Specific details regarding food and lodging can be obtained by writing to the above address.

DIRECTIONS TO THE SHRINE

National Shrine of Our Lady of Guadalupe, in Allentown, is located about forty miles north of Philadelphia.

FROM PHILADELPHIA

Take Rte. 9 north to Rte. 22 east, then take the Fullerton exit. * Take Fullerton south to Allen Street. Go west on Allen Street to Ridge Avenue.

FROM THE EAST

Take I-78 west to Rte. 22 west, then take the Fullerton exit. Follow the directions at * just above.

FROM HARRISBURG AND POINTS WEST

Take I-81 east, then I-78 east to Rte. 22 east. Exit at the Fullerton exit. Follow the directions at * above.

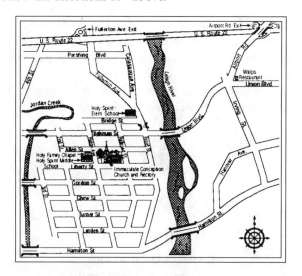

FOR FIRST-TIME PILGRIMS

Today pilgrims come to the National Shrine Center in renewed devotion. Every Sunday afternoon at 3:00 P.M. the historic church, founded in 1857 by Saint John Neumann (then bishop of Philadelphia), is the scene of rosary and litany recitations honoring Our Lady, and asking the special blessings of the Marian Year. Bishop of Allentown, Thomas J. Welsh, has designated the Church of the Immaculate Conception as a place of pilgrimage for the Marian Year. In addition, the rosary, a novena, and Mass are said every Monday morning at 7:45 A.M.

OF SPECIAL INTEREST

In the portrait that appeared miraculously on the inside of Juan Diego's *tilma*, Our Lady is pregnant. Because the Aztecs believed in human sacrifice, it is believed that Our Lady's mission was to lead the Aztec Indians to the Catholic faith and thereby end this practice. In today's world, Our Lady of Guadalupe is called the Patroness of the Pro-Life Movement, and her shrine has been called a temple of prayer in reparation for abortion. A popular pro-life prayer follows:

Lord Jesus Christ, Son of God, in you we adore the eternal origin of all life. Born of the Father before all time, you were born of the Virgin Mary in time. In your humanity and person you sanctified motherhood from the first instant of conception through all stages, for our salvation. Recall all people to these divine blessings, to appreciate the unborn as persons and to enlighten every human being coming into this world. In your mercy avert your just anger from the enemies of life, to allow God's infants to give him glory and to be crowned with the heavenly life of grace. From the cross you called, "Behold your Mother." Amen.

National Shrine of Our Lady of Mount Carmel

CARMELITE FRIARS
MIDDLETOWN, NEW YORK

The magnificent main chapel at the National Shrine of Our Lady of Mount Carmel.
(Anthony F. Chiffolo)

Throughout time, prayer and the Carmelites have been synonymous, and their devotion to Mary has inspired them in their work as missionaries, chaplains, teachers, and pastors. The Carmelite Friars have contributed greatly to the spiritual life and holiness of the Church, especially as active contemplatives.

The National Shrine of Our Lady of Mount Carmel was founded to encourage and perpetuate devotion to Mary and her scapular under the special title of Our Lady of Mount Carmel. The Carmelite Friars welcome pilgrims to the beautiful shrine, where they will find a place of witness to the importance and centrality of prayer in their lives and have an opportunity to deepen their commitment to God and devotion to Our Lady.

PRAYER TO OUR LADY OF MOUNT CARMEL

O beautiful Flower of Carmel, most fruitful vine, splendor of heaven, holy and singular, who brought forth the Son of God, still ever remaining a pure virgin, assist me in this necessity. O Star of the Sea, help and protect me. Show me that you are my Mother. Patroness of all who wear the scapular, pray for us! Hope of all who die wearing the scapular, pray for us! O sweet heart of Mary, be our salvation. Amen.

ABOUT THE SHRINE

During World War II the shrine was established at the Carmelite Church of Our Lady of the Scapular at Mount Carmel, and the work of the Friars centered around supplying members of the armed forces with scapulars. Today, devotion to Mary at the shrine includes daily devotions, special holy day celebrations, novenas, rosary processions, days of prayer, and Christian fellowship. There are many activities in which pilgrims may participate, or they may seek quiet times of personal reflection.

The magnificent main chapel is dedicated to Our Lady of Mount Carmel; here, pilgrims celebrate liturgy, attend musical programs, or pray quietly. The beautiful stained-glass windows are inspirational as well as decorative. They honor the great Saint Patrick, a reminder of the Irish roots of the Carmelite Province of Saint Elias. The beautiful and peaceful cloisters overlook the grounds and pond where pilgrims may walk in quiet contemplation and enjoy the peaceful surroundings of nature. A beautiful outdoor shrine honoring Our Lady of Mount Carmel is often the scene of outdoor rosary processions and recitations and special celebrations. Additional shrines include the Infant of Prague; Saint Thérèse, the Little Flower; and Our Lady of Knock, commemorating her apparition in Knock, Ireland, in 1879.

SHRINE INFORMATION

National Shrine of Our Lady of Mount Carmel
P.O. Box 868
Carmelite Drive
Middletown, NY 10940-0868
(914) 344-0876

TOURIST INFORMATION

There are no restaurants or overnight accommodations available at the shrine; however, every attempt is made to help pilgrims find lodging in the nearby area. Group pilgrimages may make luncheon reservations in advance. Specific information can be obtained by contacting the shrine at the above address.

DIRECTIONS TO THE SHRINE

National Shrine of Our Lady of Mount Carmel in Middletown is located about fifty miles northwest of downtown Manhattan.

BY AUTO FROM THE NORTH

Take the New York State Thruway south to exit 17 (Newburgh). After the tollbooth follow the signs to I-84. Take I-84 west to exit 3W (Middletown). (Do not take exit 4 Middletown.) After exiting, make a right turn onto Rte. 17M west to the third traffic light. Turn left at the traffic light onto County Road 78. * Bear right at the first intersection and continue over the railroad tracks to the next traffic light. Make a right at the traffic light onto Wawayanda Ave. The National Shrine is a half mile on the left (Carmelite Center). Make the first left onto Carmelite Drive.

FROM THE SOUTH

Take the New York State Thruway north to exit 16 (Harriman). After exiting from the tollbooth, proceed west on Rte. 17. Take exit 121W (which is I-84 west). Take I-84 west to exit 3W (Middletown). (Do not take exit 4 Middletown.) After exiting, make a right turn onto Rte. 17M west to the third traffic light. Turn left at the traffic light onto County Road 78. Follow the directions at * just above.

FROM THE WEST

Take I-84 east to exit 3W (Middletown). Proceed to the third traffic light. Turn left at the traffic light onto County Road 78. Follow the directions at * above.

FROM THE EAST

Take I-84 west to exit 3W (Middletown). Proceed to the third traffic light. Turn left at the traffic light onto County Road 78. Follow the directions at * above.

BY BUS

Contact the Shortline Bus Line at (914) 343-3903.

BY RAIL

Contact the Metro North train at (800) 638-7646. From the train station, contact Middletown Taxi at (914) 343-8300.

FOR FIRST-TIME PILGRIMS

The shrine is open year-round and offers individual or group pilgrims an ideal opportunity for a day of prayer and Christian fellowship. Visitors may participate in daily and Sunday liturgies, days of recollection, novenas, and celebrations for special Carmelite feast days, rosary processions, the sacrament of reconciliation, and spiritual direction. All programs are conducted in both English and Spanish and promote the spirituality of prayer, reflection, meditation, and devotion to Mary. Mass is celebrated weekdays at 11:30 A.M. and on Sunday at noon. Group pilgrimages may arrange for special scheduling in advance. Pilgrims are also invited to visit the Renewal Center and the gift shop.

Our Lady of Good Voyage

OUR LADY'S CHAPEL
NEW BEDFORD, MASSACHUSETTS

The Shrine of Our Lady of Good Voyage commemorates the apparition of the Blessed Virgin to three fishermen, all of whose names were

Our Lady of Good Voyage, carried in procession by the fishermen of New Bedford, in commemoration of her assistance to all seafarers. *(Maximilian M. Warnisher, F.I.)*

John, off the coast of Cuba near the village of Cobre in the year 1600. In danger of shipwreck during a sudden, violent storm, they called upon Mary to save them. Suddenly, through her intercession, the storm died down, the sun began to shine, and the sea became perfectly tranquil. While rowing to shore, the three seafarers spied a luminous object following them, and upon rowing toward it discovered a small image of Our Lady exactly as she had appeared to them during the storm. This image was enshrined in the village church and is still venerated in Cuba as the Virgin of Charity of Cobre and the patroness of the country. It is a larger replica of this image of the Blessed Virgin Mary that is venerated here in New Bedford at Our Lady's Chapel.

PRAYER TO THE VIRGIN OF CHARITY

Remember, O most loving Virgin Mary, Star of the Sea, never was it heard that anyone who turned to you for help was left unaided. Inspired by this confidence, though burdened by my sins, I run to your protection, for you are my Mother. O Mother of the Word of God, do not despise my words of pleading, but be merciful and hear my prayer. Amen.

SHRINE INFORMATION

Marian Friary of Our Lady, Queen of the Seraphic Order
Our Lady's Chapel
600 Pleasant Street
New Bedford, MA 02741
(508) 996-8274

TOURIST INFORMATION

Specific information regarding restaurants and hotel accommodations can be obtained by writing to the above address.

DIRECTIONS TO THE SHRINE

New Bedford is about forty-five miles south of Boston, and the Shrine of Our Lady of Good Voyage is located in the historic district of this fishing port associated with whaling and with Herman Melville's classic *Moby Dick*. It is directly opposite City Hall and the main public library, a few blocks from the Seamen's Bethel (also in *Moby Dick*) and from the whaling museum.

OF SPECIAL INTEREST

Each year, on the second-to-last weekend of September, the feast of Our Lady of Good Voyage is held at the Friary Church of Our Lady, Queen of the Seraphic Order (Our Lady's Chapel) in New Bedford. This feast honors the Blessed Virgin Mary as patroness of fishermen and all seafarers and, indeed, of all Christians on pilgrimage through this life to heaven. The lives of fishermen and seafarers are difficult and challenging for themselves and their families. But especially during times of economic decline and hardship, this feast is an opportunity for them, and all of us as a Christian community, to implore the motherly assistance of their patroness, the Blessed Virgin Mary of Good Voyage. All Christians, especially those who make their living on the sea, are encouraged to take part in this festival and to make of it what it is intended to be: a time of pilgrimage, prayer, remembrance, and thanksgiving to her for the maternal care she has bestowed, and is ever ready to bestow, on those who turn to her in their need.

Our Lady of the Highway

OUR LADY OF THE HOLY ANGELS PARISH
LITTLE FALLS, NEW JERSEY

The devotion to Our Lady of the Highway dates from the early centuries of the Church—to the Shrine of Santa Maria della Strada: Holy Mary of the Street at Rome. Saint Ignatius of Loyola practiced devotion to Our Lady under this title. We honor Mary as Our Lady of the Highway when we consider her various journeys: the Visitation, the journey from Nazareth to Bethlehem, the Presentation, the Flight into Egypt, and the Way of the Cross. Today, this title has new significance in view of the dangers and death present on the highway. Many thousands meet death annually on the roads, and many others

We honor Mary as Our Lady of the Highway when we consider the dangerous travels she undertook and invoke her aid during our journeying. *(Anthony F. Chiffolo)*

are injured. But whenever we are in peril of affliction, Mary is there under some special title to provide a model of God's protection for us. Let us then seek the protection of God who protected Mary on her many journeys. Let us ask God to guide us in his way as we go on our way.

PRAYER OF PROTECTION
FOR A TRAVELER

Gracious God, you who guided Mary on her many journeys, guide and protect us as we go on our way. Amen.

SHRINE INFORMATION

Our Lady of the Highway Shrine
Our Lady of the Holy Angels Parish
473 Main Street
Little Falls, NJ 07424
(201) 256-5200

TOURIST INFORMATION

Restaurant and hotel accommodations are readily available in the nearby area. Some suggestions for overnight lodging include Holiday Inn (Rte. 46, Totowa), Howard Johnson (Rte. 3, Clifton), and Radisson Hotel (Rte. 46, Fairfield).

DIRECTIONS TO THE SHRINE

About fifteen miles west of Manhattan, Our Lady of the Highway Shrine is located on the front lawn of Our Lady of the Holy Angels Parish at 80 Newark-Pompton Turnpike (Rte. 23) in Little Falls.

FROM RTE. 46 EAST OR WEST

Take the McBride Avenue exit coming from either direction. McBride Avenue turns into Paterson Avenue. Take it to the end. * Make a right onto Main Street and go through two stoplights over the railroad tracks, and the church is on your left-hand side.

FROM RTE. 23 NORTH

Take Rte. 23 south, following the signs to Verona. Pass Willowbrook on your right, and go over a small bridge. At the next light, make a left onto Main Street and take the second right into the driveway.

FROM I-80 (DELAWARE WATER GAP)

Take I-80 east to Rte. 46 east. Exit at McBride Avenue, and at the bottom of the ramp bear right onto Paterson Avenue (McBride changes to Paterson Avenue in Little Falls). Take it to the end. Follow the directions at * above.

FROM THE GEORGE WASHINGTON BRIDGE

Take I-80 west to Rte. 23 south (Verona). Pass Willowbrook on your right, and go over a small bridge. At the next light, make a left onto Main Street and take the second right into the driveway.

FROM THE GARDEN STATE PARKWAY

Take exit 153 (Rte. 3 and Rte. 46). Route 3 feeds into Route 46 west. Exit at McBride Avenue. Make a left at the bottom of the ramp onto Paterson Avenue. Take it to the end. Follow the directions at * above.

FROM THE LINCOLN TUNNEL

Take Rte. 3 west to Rte. 46 west. Exit at McBride Avenue. Make a left at the bottom of the ramp onto Paterson Avenue. Take it to the end. Follow the directions at * above.

FOR FIRST-TIME PILGRIMS

The Shrine of Our Lady of the Highway is open to the public at all times—twenty-four hours a day, seven days a week. There are no special novenas or pilgrimage dates.

Our Lady of the Highways
OBLATES OF SAINT FRANCIS DE SALES
CHILDS, MARYLAND

Though you are tossed on the waves and amid the winds of many troubles, always look up to heaven and say to Our Lord: "O God, it is for you that I voyage and sail. Be my guide and my pilot."
SAINT FRANCIS DE SALES

A few year ago the founder of the Oblate Helpers' Guild, Fr. John Fuqua, had the inspiration to invoke Mary as the patron of the millions who daily place themselves behind the wheel. After a horrible accident on I-95, just a few yards from the Oblate Community, Father

Fuqua was determined to find some tangible way to remind motorists to be more responsible. He was inspired to ask Mary for help—after all, she had been a traveler all her life. So his reminder took the form of a beautiful statue on the hilly grounds. He named her Our Lady of the Highways.

PRAYER TO OUR LADY OF THE HIGHWAYS

May my traveling
be to the honor and glory
of your Divine Son.
Enlighten my way
and protect me on this journey.
Bring me back home safe
in mind, body, and soul.
Through Christ, your Son.
Amen.

ABOUT THE SHRINE

Father Fuqua did not "invent" the title "Our Lady of the Highways." The Blessed Mother has been honored under this name

Our Lady of the Highways encourages pilgrims to pray for all travelers and to be responsible drivers. *(Our Lady of the Highways)*

for many years, and a number of shrines and parishes in Europe and a few here in the United States honor her in this way. A couple of years after the statue was erected, Fr. John J. Conmy, O.S.F.S., landscaped the hillside and planted shrubbery in the shape of a cross flanked by the letters *V* and *J*. These symbols, bright yellow and flaming red in the fall, can be clearly seen from the highway. The letters stand for "Vive Jesus" ("Live, Jesus"), an expression Saint Francis de Sales placed at the head of all his letters to remind people to live a life in union with God.

In 1986 the statue was replaced with a taller, marble statue that was dedicated on October 11 of that year. In an effort to make this highway the safest in our nation, the Oblates continue to encourage the thousands of members all across the country to help pass the word around and get others to pray for all travelers and be responsible drivers.

SHRINE INFORMATION

Rev. Richard DeLillio, O.S.F.S.
Our Lady of the Highways
P.O. Box 87
Childs, MD 21916-0087
(410) 398-3057

TOURIST INFORMATION

The Shrine of Our Lady of the Highways is located in rural Cecil County on the eastern shore of Maryland. It is beautiful any time of the year, but it is spectacular in the spring. The nearest airports are Baltimore-Washington International to the southwest and Philadelphia to the north. There is no direct access from I-95, but the shrine is easy to find. There are motels of different price ranges at the exit from I-95.

DIRECTIONS TO THE SHRINE

Our Lady of the Highways is located about forty miles northeast of Baltimore. Take I-95 to the Elkton, Maryland, exit, go south on 279, and turn right at the fourth light. Drive two miles along MD 545 (Blue Ball Road). Turn right at the sign that says, "Oblate Retreat Center" and follow the signs for parking. Anyone at the "Reverend John J. Fuqua Center" for the "de Sales Center" will be glad to show you around.

FOR FIRST-TIME PILGRIMS

Besides living quarters for older Oblates, the property also houses an assisted-living facility and a retreat center. It is the home of Fr. John Conmy, O.S.F.S., the National Assistant of the Marian Institute of Saint Francis de Sales, who for many years was provincial of the Oblates. He is not only spiritual director to many but also an avid horticulturist. Though he's in his eighties, you can still find him planting, trimming, and pruning, lovingly enhancing this extensive property. Mass is offered on the holidays when travel is heaviest in the Our Lady of Light Chapel.

OF SPECIAL INTEREST

Today, many vehicles—cars, trucks, buses, even boats—carry on the windshield or dashboard a small sticker that shows the image of the

Lady on the hillside and the words "Our Lady of the Highways, protect all travelers."

Truck drivers use the shrine as a reference point. If you listen to CB calls in the area, you often hear them mention the "Stone Lady."

Many people have written to Father Fuqua, and to the priests who took up his work after his death, to relate various stories or experiences they had while driving. Many are convinced that Our Lady of the Highways has in some way protected them or saved them from serious accidents.

Our Lady of Victory Basilica and National Shrine

FATHER BAKER'S HOMES OF CHARITY
LACKAWANNA, NEW YORK

The Basilica of Our Lady of Victory stands as a tangible symbol of one man's faith in God and his devotion to Mary. The Rev. Nelson Henry Baker, familiarly known as "Father Baker," crowned the sixty years of his priesthood and charity work with a magnificent shrine honoring his spiritual helpmate. Father Baker credited Mary with the phenomenal success of his work, which saved thousands of infant lives; housed, fed, and educated tens of thousands of orphaned or troubled boys; and provided aid to multitudes of adults in hard economic times. Father Baker had a lifelong devotion to Mary as his victorious Lady. Without hesitation, he gave her credit for

Built in fourteenth- and fifteenth-century Renaissance style, Our Lady of Victory Basilica and National Shrine reminds pilgrims that Mary is the perfect conduit to God's mercy and love. (Our Lady of Victory Basilica and National Shrine)

all his success in helping the poor and afflicted. "I'm just her agent," he stoutly maintained.

PRAYER TO OUR LADY OF VICTORY

Victorious Lady, thou who has ever such powerful influence with thy Divine Son, in conquering the hardest of hearts, intercede for those for whom we pray, that their hearts being softened by the rays of Divine Grace, they may return to the unity of the true Faith, through Christ, our Lord. Amen.

ABOUT THE SHRINE

The basilica is built in fourteenth- and fifteenth-century Renaissance style. The French baroque interior decoration utilizes light tones in shades of ivory, light brown, and blue to harmonize with the marble colors. The most prominent exterior features of the basilica are its copper-topped twin towers and a huge copper dome, 165 feet high, cited at the time as second in size only to the dome in the nation's Capitol Building. Four winged copper angels, each eighteen feet high, raise their trumpets in four directions around the dome.

At the main entrance, a domed niche houses a twelve-foot-high statue of Our Lady of Victory weighing eight tons. Two large colonnades flank the exterior sides of the shrine. Topping each is a marble sculpture of a group of children. One honors the Sisters of St. Joseph who have staffed the institutions since 1856. The other, ordered by his assistant as a surprise, depicts Father Baker with a group of boys.

In the vestibule, under a rococo-style ceiling, hang three elaborate bronze chandeliers, facsimiles of those in the Holy House of Loreto in Italy. They illuminate four life-size angels and four sculpture groupings. These last depict the Precious Blood of Jesus, the Blessed Mother of the Rosary, Mary of the Scapular with Saint Simon Stock, and the Holy Family.

Huge bronze doors, of which there are more than eighty in the basilica, swing open to reveal the church proper. Pews of rare African mahogany, seating one thousand, rest on a gently sloping floor allowing all worshipers an unobstructed view of the high altar. Its focal point is a nine-foot statue of Our Lady of Victory, which was personally blessed by Pope Pius XI before its shipment from Rome. A gracefully swirled marble canopy protects her and supports a large gold cross held aloft by four angels. Overhead, a bright blue dome depicts the Holy Spirit. The tabernacle is framed by folds of marble drapery held apart by angels. Red marble obtained from the Pyrenees Mountains forms swirled columns patterned after those in St. Peter's Basilica in Rome. On the sanctuary ceiling, a large mural represents "the Queen of All Saints."

Magnificent sculptures, including the fourteen Stations of the Cross, and numerous altars grace the church interior. The most elaborate and challenging work of art appears in the Great Dome. The oil painting in the dome celebrates the Assumption into Heaven and Coronation of the Blessed Virgin Mary. A blue background reveals numerous figures sharing in Mary's triumph: an angelic host who carries her heavenward, choirs of angels, the Twelve Apostles, and three archangels. "There are a thousand angels in the basilica," Father Baker once said. And everywhere one looks, an angel's face is likely to look back. Their presence is not merely decorative. Scripture teaches that angels are the highest of God's creatures, pure in spirit, existing solely to glorify God. The angels remind us that for all its beauty, even its dedication to Our Lady of Victory, the basilica is meant primarily for God's praise and glory—with Mary as the perfect conduit to his mercy and love.

SHRINE INFORMATION

Our Lady of Victory Institutions
780 Ridge Road
Lackawanna, NY 14218
(716) 828-9648
fax (716) 828-9604

TOURIST INFORMATION

Information for dining and overnight accommodations may be obtained by contacting the Greater Buffalo Convention and Visitor's Bureau at 1-800-BUFFALO, or by writing to 617 Main Street, Buffalo, NY 14203, or via e-mail at info@buffalocvb.org

DIRECTIONS TO THE SHRINE

Our Lady of Victory Basilica and National Shrine is about five miles southeast of downtown Buffalo.

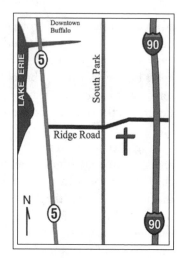

FROM CANADA (QEW) AND DOWNTOWN BUFFALO

Take Rte. 5 (Skyway) west and exit at Ridge Road.

FROM THE NORTH (NIAGARA FALLS)

Take I-90 south to Rte. 5 (Skyway) west, and exit at Ridge Road. Or take I-290 east to the New York State Thruway (I-90) west, and exit at 55 (Lackawanna/Ridge Road).

FROM THE EAST (ROCHESTER)

Take the New York State Thruway (I-90) west to exit 55 (Lackawanna/ Ridge Road).

FROM THE SOUTH (ERIE)

Take the New York State Thruway (I-90) east to exit 55 (Lackawanna/ Ridge Road). Or take Rte. 20 to Rte. 62 (South Park Avenue).

FOR FIRST-TIME PILGRIMS

Our Lady of Victory Basilica and National Shrine conducts open tours every Sunday at 1:00 P.M., or appointments can be arranged by calling (716) 828-9444. Mass is celebrated daily at 7:30 and 8:30 A.M. and 12:10 P.M.; Saturday at 4:30 P.M.; and on Sundays at 8:00 and 10:00 A.M. (folk Mass), noon (choir), and 4:30 P.M.

OF SPECIAL INTEREST

Father Baker's original rooms are reconstructed in the basement of the shrine. They include his furniture, books, and wall hangings. A glass cabinet displays his various personal belongings as well as family and other photographs. An illuminated glass case contains a plaster death mask of the saintly priest. Vintage newspapers carry headlines of his death on July 29, 1936, at the age of ninety-five.

Shrine of the Miraculous Icon of Our Lady of Zhyrovytsi

CYRIL AND METHODIUS
UKRAINIAN CATHOLIC CHURCH
OLYPHANT, PENNSYLVANIA

More than five hundred years ago, in the 1470s, four shepherd boys were tending their flocks in the outskirts of the little village of Zhyrovytsi in northeastern Ukraine. Attracted by brilliant rays of light from a nearby wild pear tree, the boys approached. As they got closer, the rays faded and the shepherds beheld in the branches of the tree a beautiful icon of Our Lady holding the Baby Jesus. They removed the icon from the tree and entrusted it to their landlord, Alexander Soltan, a relative of Joseph Soltan, archbishop-metropolitan of Kiev.

The amazed landlord locked the icon in a wooden chest for safekeeping. The next day, wishing to show the icon to some visiting guests, he opened the chest and found it empty. At almost the

The Shrine of the Miraculous Icon of Our Lady of Zhyrovytsi holds a replica of the miraculous icon found in the Ukraine more than five hundred years ago. *(Shrine of the Miraculous Icon of Our Lady of Zhyrovytsi)*

same time, the shepherd boys again reported that they had seen the icon in the same tree. Alexander Soltan and others considered this to be a clear sign that the Blessed Mother wished to remain and be venerated on that spot. So Soltan built a church in which to enshrine the icon.

In subsequent years, veneration of the icon spread widely. Its devotion reached even to Rome in the small Church of Sts. Sergius and Bacchus on the Piazza Madonna dei Monti, which was assigned by the pope to the metropolitan of Kiev in 1639. It was not until 1718, however, that some workmen discovered a well-preserved icon embedded in the plaster of the church's interior wall. The icon was none other than that of Our Lady of Zhyrovytsi. How it came to be there is a mystery for which no historical record is available. The remarkable preservation of the icon was considered extraordinary. Veneration of Our Lady of Zhyrovytsi became established or re-established in this Church of Sts. Sergius and Bacchus in Rome. Many graces and miraculous cures have been attributed to this icon by pilgrims who have visited it there.

Fr. Michael Guryansky, pastor of St. Cyril's in Olyphant from 1920 to 1935, had a great devotion to the Blessed Virgin Mary. His dream was to build a shrine in the front yard of the rectory. When the present school was being built in 1926, the plans provided for installing a water line from the school plumbing into the rectory yard in preparation for two fountains that would have graced the shrine. The premature death of Father Guryansky in 1935 did not permit him to realize his plans.

However, two women of the parish, Mrs. Lubow Swallow and Mrs. Nellie Wysochansky, kept the dream of the shrine alive in their memories long after Father Guryansky's death. In 1952 they informed Msgr. Stephen Hrynuck, the newly appointed pastor, of Father Guryansky's dream. Monsignor Hrynuck eagerly embraced the idea of fulfilling Father Guryansky's dream for a special reason, namely, to thank God for peace and unity in the parish following a recent period of dissension among parish factions. The solemn dedication and blessing of the shrine took place on May 18, 1980.

PRAYER TO OUR LADY OF ZHYROVYTSI

Hail, O Blessed Virgin Mary, Mother of God, who deigned to appear to a group of poor shepherd boys in the form of an icon in a pear tree in Zhyrovytsi. Most Holy Immaculate Virgin, Our Lady of Zhyrovytsi, who art the Mother of my Lord, the Queen of Heaven and Earth, Mother of divine grace, Virgin most merciful, to you I come both sinful and sorrowful. To you I render humble homage and thank you, O Mother most admirable. I promise to serve you always and do all in my power to make others love you.

I place in you all my hope; I confide my salvation to your care. Through intercession with your Divine Son enlighten my mind, purify my heart, and fill my soul with the graces I stand in most need of now. Accept me for your servant, and protect me under your blue mantle, O Mother of Mercy. I humbly beseech you, O Mother most powerful, to obtain for me the graces and favors I now seek, if they be beneficial to my immortal soul, and the souls for whom I pray. (Here mention private petitions.) By your power obtain for me the strength of will to resist all temptations until death. Dear Lady of Zhyrovytsi, by the love which you did bear to God, I beseech you always to help me, especially at the hour of my death. Do not abandon me, I implore you, until you see me safe in heaven, blessing you and singing your praises for all eternity. Amen.

ABOUT THE SHRINE

The stonework of the shrine is of Georgian marble. The main wall of the shrine rises eleven feet high, and at the top is a semicircular arch. Seated on the top center of this arch is a single-bar cross of granite on the face of which is etched in fine gold foil a Byzantine three-bar cross.

Just below the icon that is embedded in the face of the main wall is a gray granite slab that serves as an altar top. This top is supported by two granite pillars on the left and right sides that slant back at a forty-five-degree angle to connect to the base of the shrine wall. Recessed step-shelving to the left and right of this altar in the lower part of the extended wall base serves as a repository for votive candles.

In the base wall just below the altar slab is a gold sunburst mosaic that has a semblance of a two-bar cross in its center. The gold sunburst is set in a field of blue mosaic chips.

The shrine edifice sits on a large patio that is connected to the Grant Street sidewalk by a shrub-lined concrete walkway. Along the Grant Street sidewalk is a three-foot-high wall of Georgian granite pierced by an entrance to the walkway to the shrine patio.

Just forward to the left and right of the shrine wall, situated on the patio at a forty-five-degree angle to the shrine, are two rectangular granite enclosures about three feet high housing electrically illuminated fountains. Floodlights illuminate the entire shrine at night and bring out the beauty of the blue and gold mosaic chips in the icon. The backside of the shrine is surrounded by an elegantly trimmed green wall of stately pine trees. A single marble bench graces each side of the front part of the patio. The grounds surrounding the side and front of the patio are beautified by a lush carpet of green grass interspersed with beds of green plantings of seasonal flowers and bushes.

The icon itself shows Our Lady adorned in a red gown, covered by a deep blue tunic from her head down. In her right arm she holds the Infant Jesus clothed in a white robe. Similar gold crowns with embedded pearls or white stones and a small cross on top adorn their heads. The Greek letters for Jesus Christ and Mary, Mother of God, appear respectively to the left and right of the figures. Inscribed in an oval ring around the figures are the immortal words of the "Hymn to the Blessed Virgin" taken from the liturgy of Saint John Chrysostom: "More honorable than the cherubim and by far more glorious than the seraphim; ever a virgin, you gave birth to God the Word, O true Mother of God, we magnify you." Beneath the icon in the gray granite support slab are engraved the words "Miraculous Icon, Our Lady of Zhyrovytsi, Most Holy Mother of God, save us."

SHRINE INFORMATION

Shrine of the Miraculous Icon of Our Lady of Zhyrovytsi
Cyril and Methodius Ukrainian Catholic Church
135 River Street
Olyphant, PA 18447
(717) 489-2271

TOURIST INFORMATION

Specific information regarding restaurants and overnight lodging can be obtained by contacting the shrine at the above address.

DIRECTIONS TO THE SHRINE

Olyphant is just on the northeastern outskirts of Scranton. The Shrine of the Miraculous Icon of Our Lady of Zhyrovytsi is located in a specially built outdoor shrine in the rear of Sts. Cyril and Methodius Ukrainian Catholic Church. It can best be reached by taking I-81 north to Rte. 6 northeast, to Rte. 347 southeast. The Church of Sts. Cyril and Methodius is a left-hand turn on River Street, immediately after you leave Dickson City and cross Main Street, the railroad tracks, and Hull Creek.

OF SPECIAL INTEREST

Many people of the area have developed a special devotion for Our Lady of Zhyrovytsi and can be seen visiting, praying, and lighting votive candles at the altar of the shrine at almost any hour of day or night. Automobiles pause on Grant Street in front of the shrine as the driver or its occupants whisper a quick, silent Hail Mary to Our Lady; or as on one occasion the rear door of an auto opened to reveal a tiny child rush up the walk to Our Lady's Shrine, place a flower on the altar, and throw a kiss to the Mother of the Infant Jesus, cradled tenderly in her arms. And not uncommon have been the somewhat loud visits made late at night by those persons who have spent an enjoyable evening at one of the local taverns.

Whoever the individual, whatever the intention, whatever the situation, Our Lady of Zhyrovytsi is always present, enshrined in a beautiful blue and gold mosaic icon, waiting, listening, interceding, and bringing consolation to all who seek her aid. No records exist or can ever be kept of how often she has satisfied the various intentions presented to her—for recovery of health, restoration of a broken home, employment, safety of children, the overcoming of evil habits, and so on. Those who have sought her intercession know the favors she has bestowed. As for the rest of us, it is a test of our faith and belief in the intercessory power of the Mother of God, under whatever image or icon she is represented, including that of the Miraculous Icon of Our Lady of Zhyrovytsi.

Shrine of Our Lady of Grace

MISSIONARY OBLATES OF MARY IMMACULATE
COLEBROOK, NEW HAMPSHIRE

The Missionary Oblates of Mary Immaculate of the Northern United States Province established a minor seminary (high school) in

Colebrook, New Hampshire, during the fall of 1922. For nineteen consecutive years young men from all sections of New England and part of New York State journeyed to this far-northern haven to begin the many years of study required to attain the religious priesthood. In 1941, when these facilities proved inadequate for the housing of all prospective Oblate candidates, this seminary was transferred to larger quarters in Bucksport, Maine, and the Colebrook establishment was transformed into a novitiate offering an intense year of religious training to young adults aspiring to the Oblate priesthood or brotherhood.

The Shrine of Our Lady of Grace commemorates the Virgin's enthronement as Queen of Mountains and Queen of Men. *(Shrine of Our Lady of Grace)*

In 1947, as the twenty-fifth anniversary of the Oblates' arrival in Colebrook neared, the Rev. Louis S. Desruisseaux, O.M.I., superior at the novitiate, envisioned erecting a monument to Our Lady of Grace, Patroness of the Novitiate, in heartfelt gratitude for the quarter century of vocational blessings that the Missionary Oblates had experienced here. Work began on April 19, 1948, with the help of priests, brothers, and lay volunteers. On October 10, 1948, more than three thousand pilgrims swarmed to Colebrook.

Most Rev. Matthew F. Brade, bishop of Manchester, solemnly blessed the Statue of Our Lady of Grace and officially dedicated Mary's newest shrine. All had come to witness the Virgin's enthronement as Queen of Mountains and Queen of Men. Mary's universal role was properly extolled that day!

PRAYER TO OUR MOTHER OF THE WORD INCARNATE

Virgin most holy, Mother of the Word Incarnate, treasurer of graces, and refuge of us poor sinners, we fly to your motherly affection with lively faith, and we beg of you the grace ever to do the will of God. Into your most holy hands we commit the keeping of our hearts, asking you for health of soul and body, in the certain hope that you, our most loving mother, will hear our prayer.

ABOUT THE SHRINE

The focal point of the shrine grounds is a twenty-one-foot pedestal built of field stones on which sits the white Carrara-marble statue of Our Lady of Grace. Other major additions to the shrine include a permanent Rock of Ages granite altar, an outdoor Way of the Cross with the fourteen stations, the fifteen permanent mysteries of the rosary, a giant replica of the World Mission Rosary, Family Rosary Lake, and numerous statues located throughout the shrine grounds.

SHRINE INFORMATION

Shrine of Our Lady of Grace
RR1 Box 521
Colebrook, NH 03576-9535
(603) 237-5511

TOURIST INFORMATION

A number of hotel, motel, and cabin accommodations are available and can be contacted for reservations and directions to the shrine:

- The Colebrook House: (603) 237-5521
- Northern Comfort Motel: (603) 237-4440
- Colebrook Country Club Motel and Restaurant: (603) 237-5566

- Diamond Peaks Motel and Country Store: (603) 237-5104
- Rippling Brook Cabins: (603) 237-5753
- Columbia Cabins: (603) 237-8630
- Mohawk Cottages: (603) 237-4310

DIRECTIONS TO THE SHRINE

The Shrine of Our Lady of Grace is located 200 hundred miles north of Boston, Massachusetts, and 165 miles north of Manchester, New Hampshire.

FROM SOUTHERN NEW ENGLAND

Take I-93 north to Rte. 3 north to Colebrook.

FROM MAINE

Take Rte. 26 south, then Rte. 2 west to Rte. 3 north.

FROM VERMONT

Take Rtes. 114, 105, or 2 to Rte. 3 north.

FROM CANADA

Take Rte. 147 to Vermont, then Rte. 114 south to Rte. 105. Then take Rte. 3 north to Colebrook.

FOR FIRST-TIME PILGRIMS

The Shrine of Our Lady of Grace begins its annual pilgrimages on Mother's Day (in May), continuing throughout the summer until the second Sunday in October. From May to October, Mass is celebrated at 7:30 A.M. daily for the community in the residence chapel and at 11:00 A.M. daily at the shrine chapel. Sunday Mass is celebrated at 11:00 A.M. and Holy Hour at 3:00 P.M. Pilgrims to the shrine, in discovering the peace and the beauty of nature where this shrine rests, take the time to relax and discover God in his creation and the motherly warmth of Our Lady who looks over her children.

OF SPECIAL INTEREST

In 1976 the White Mountain Motorcycle Club of Berlin, New Hampshire, began hosting an Annual Blessing of Motorcycles at Our Lady of

Grace. Throughout the years, several members from this club and some from other motorcycle clubs have donated time, energy, and finances toward the further development of the shrine. This group revamped the entire lighting system, installing underground wiring everywhere on the shrine grounds to ensure an unobstructed view of all monuments. On June 22, 1986, the club donated and dedicated an imposing monument titled "Motorcyclists in Prayer." And on June 23, 1991, members of the club unveiled a stirring Memorial to Military Personnel from the United States who served in Operation Desert Storm, especially to those who sacrificed their lives to the cause of freedom in this conflict.

$$\frac{+\ \|\ +}{+\ \|\ +}$$

Shrine of Our Lady of Martyrs

AURIESVILLE, NEW YORK

Auriesville is the site of the Mohawk Indians' palisaded village of Ossemenon. It was here that Fr. Isaac Jogues and Rene Goupil were brought in August, 1642, after their capture by the Mohawks. On September 29, 1642, Rene was killed. Father Jogues buried him in a ravine outside the village. After a year in captivity, Father Jogues escaped from the Indians. Later, he returned to the Mohawks, and he was martyred on October 18, 1646. The next day his young companion, John LaLande, was also killed.

These three martyrs, along with five other Jesuit missionaries martyred in Canada, were canonized by the Church in 1930. In 1969 Pope Paul VI appointed October 19 as the date to observe their feast throughout the world.

Kateri Tekakwitha,

The Shrine of Our Lady of Martyrs reminds pilgrims that this hallowed ground is sanctified by the blood of Catholic martyrs. *(Shrine of Our Lady of Martyrs)*

proclaimed "blessed" by Pope John Paul II in 1980, was born here at Auriesville in 1656 to a Christian Algonquin mother and a Mohawk chief, but she was orphaned at the age of three. She was eleven when other Jesuit missionaries came to her people. Baptized in 1676 near Fonda, where the National Tekakwitha Shrine now stands, she left the next year to join other Christian Mohawks at Caughnawaga on the St. Lawrence River.

PRAYER TO MARY, QUEEN OF MARTYRS

Mary, most holy Virgin and Queen of Martyrs, would that I could be in heaven to contemplate the honors showered upon you by the ever-blessed Trinity and by all the hosts of heaven. But seeing that I am still a pilgrim in this vale of tears, please accept from me, your most unworthy servant and a miserable sinner, the most sincere homage and the most perfect act of submission that any human creature can make to you. On my last day come to me, as you once assisted your Divine Son, in his agony, so that I may pass from this bitter exile to share in your glory in heaven.

ABOUT THE SHRINE

Our Lady of the Martyrs Shrine was established by the Rev. Joseph Loyzance, S.J., who purchased ten acres of land in 1885. Father Loyzance was a student of the lives of the early North American missionaries and was able to determine the exact location of their martyrdom. A simple chapel on the hill was erected, and later, when the cause of their canonization was successfully concluded, the present shrine was established as a monument to these first canonized saints of North America. The various outdoor shrines and the unique Coliseum Church remind us that this hallowed ground is sanctified by the blood of zealous followers of Christ. Pope Pius XII called Auriesville "nature's own reliquary—the verdant hill that slopes up from the quiet, easy flowing river of the Mohawks."

The shrine grounds include a wood carving of Saint John LaLande and a statue of Saint Isaac Jogues carving crosses on a tree—which he did during his lonely exile. There is another statue of Blessed Kateri Tekakwitha, the first laywoman in North America to be honored as "blessed." In the ravine stands a statue that represents Saint Rene Goupil making the sign of the cross over an Indian boy. It was for this act that the missionary was martyred.

SHRINE INFORMATION

>Our Lady of the Martyrs
>Shrine of the North American Martyrs
>Auriesville, New York 12016
>(518) 853-3033

TOURIST INFORMATION

The shrine grounds have a modern cafeteria that can serve five hundred pilgrims and visitors at a single sitting. Modern motels are available in Fultonville, Fonda, Amsterdam, Johnstown, and Gloversville, all within a distance of three to ten miles of Auriesville.

DIRECTIONS TO THE SHRINE

The Shrine of the Martyrs is located in the beautiful Mohawk Valley in eastern New York State, forty miles west of Albany.

FROM THE EAST AND SOUTH

Take the New York State Thruway (I-90) west and exit at Amsterdam Interchange 27. Continue west on Rte. 5S.

FROM THE WEST

Take the New York State Thruway (I-90) east and exit at Fultonville Interchange 28. Continue east along Rte. 5S.

FROM THE NORTH

Take the Northway (I-87) south to the New York State Thruway (I-90), then take the Thruway west. Exit at Amsterdam Interchange 27. Continue west on Rte. 5S.

BY TRAIN

Amtrak trains run to Amsterdam, six miles away from Auriesville.

BY BUS

Trailways buses run to Fonda, four miles away from Auriesville.

FOR FIRST-TIME PILGRIMS

The Shrine of Our Lady of Martyrs is open May 4 through October 26. Mass is celebrated weekdays at 11:30 A.M. and 4:00 P.M., on Saturday at 4:00 P.M. and 7:30 P.M. (early July through Labor Day), and on Sunday at 9:00 and 10:30 A.M., noon, and 4:00 P.M.

Pilgrims are also invited to attend the rosary, Stations of the Cross, and Eucharistic procession at 2:30 P.M. each Sunday. Confessions are heard before each Mass, and Benediction is at 3:30 P.M. daily.

OF SPECIAL INTEREST

The Coliseum Church was opened in 1931, a year after the martyrs' canonization, and was one of the first circular churches in the United States. It can accommodate 6,500 worshipers. The altar of the Coliseum was built to resemble the palisaded barriers that usually surrounded the villages of the Mohawks and the other Iroquois nations.

$$+\!\!\parallel\!\!+$$
$$+\!\!\parallel\!\!+$$

Shrine of Our Lady of the Island

MONTFORT MISSIONARIES
EASTPORT, NEW YORK

In 1953 Mr. Crescenzo Vigliotta, Sr., donated seventy acres of land in Eastport, Long Island, to the Montfort Missionaries for a shrine to honor Mary, the Mother of God. Soon after, Mr. and Mrs. John Harrison of East Moriches donated a rock—the largest rock formation on Long Island—and the surrounding acreage overlooking Moriches Bay. It was on this rock formation that an eighteen-foot statue of the Blessed Virgin Mary was placed, overlooking the Atlantic Ocean and offering the visitor a unique view of the southern shore of Long Island.

BLESSING INVOKING OUR LADY OF THE ISLAND

May Our Lady of the Island fill your heart and your home with the love of Jesus Christ.

ABOUT THE SHRINE

Connected by a winding foot-path, the fourteen Stations of the Cross are set in the peaceful still-ness of the wooded hillside. The scene of the crucifixion of Jesus high above the pilgrim's footpath dominates the entire length of the Way of the Cross. Life-size figures in bright, natural color recreate the sacred setting of the final hours of Jesus on the hill of Calvary. A giant cross cut from rich evergreen marks the en-trance to the rosary prayer walk. One hundred and fifty juniper bushes spaced in a quarter mile circle count off each Hail Mary of the rosary, a prayer that had its origins in Europe more than ten centuries ago.

The Shrine of Our Lady of the Island offers pilgrims a peaceful setting for prayer and meditation. *(Anthony F. Chiffolo)*

SHRINE INFORMATION

Shrine of Our Lady of the Island
Montfort Missionaries
Box 26
Eastport, New York 11941
(516) 325-0661

TOURIST INFORMATION

Contact the Montfort Missionaries at the above address for specific information regarding overnight accommodations. The shrine grounds have a snack bar and picnic areas available for pilgrim use.

DIRECTIONS TO THE SHRINE

Eastport, New York, is about sixty miles east of downtown Manhat-tan. To reach the Shrine of Our Lady of the Island, take the Long Island

Expressway (I-495) east to exit 70. At the stop sign turn right. Continue for two miles to Eastport-Manor Road. Take this road a half mile to the shrine entrance.

If using the Sunrise Highway, take exit 61. Keep to the left and at the stop sign turn left. Cross over Hwy. 51 at the traffic light. The shrine is two miles on your left.

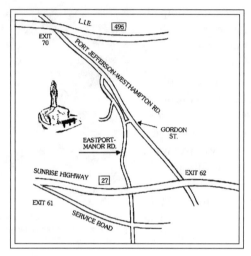

FOR FIRST-TIME PILGRIMS

The Shrine of Our Lady of the Island is open daily from 10:00 A.M. until 4:00 P.M. The grounds are open from dawn to dusk. Mass is celebrated weekdays and Saturday at 9:30 A.M. and on Sunday and holy days at 10:00 A.M. Retreat and recollection days are conducted in St. Bernadette Pilgrim Hall for parish groups and church-affiliated organizations.

The grounds are ideal for meditation or just for getting in touch with oneself in the quiet of a solitary walk. Whether spending the day at the shrine or only a few hours, pilgrims are always special guests, brothers and sisters in Christ. The Montfort Missionaries extend a cordial welcome to all pilgrims and invite them to make use of all the shrine facilities: snack bar, gift shop, lavatory conveniences, and spacious picnic areas.

OF SPECIAL INTEREST

The Montfort Missionaries are always available to meet the needs of their visitors at the Shrine of Our Lady of the Island. Founded in France more than 275 years ago, this congregation of priests and brothers is dedicated to the shrine for the purpose of giving people a better understanding of Mary, the Mother of Jesus Christ.

$$+\!\!+\!\!+$$

Shrine of Saint Mary, Our Lady of Guadalupe

ST. MARY'S CHURCH
KITTANNING, PENNSYLVANIA

According to tradition, on a cold morning in December 1531, the Blessed Virgin Mary appeared to Juan Diego, an Indian descended from the ancient Aztec civilization. Juan Diego was on his way to Mass, and he was distracted by the strange silence that replaced the sounds of the birds. Juan then heard a woman's voice calling him from a hill at Tepeyac, a hill where the Aztecs worshiped the mother of their gods. When he reached the top of Tepeyac Hill he saw a dazzling young woman in garments of salmon and bluish-green colors, encircled with rays as bright as the sun as a background. The Blessed Virgin's message was simple:

This mosaic in the Shrine of Saint Mary, Our Lady of Guadalupe tells the story of the apparition of the Virgin Mary to Juan Diego, a Native American Indian, in 1531. *(Shrine of Saint Mary, Our Lady of Guadalupe)*

I am the Holy Mary ever Virgin. I greatly desire that a church be built to me here, so that I may give all my love, compassion, and help. For I am a Compassionate Mother to you and to all of my devoted children who will call upon me with confidence. It is here I wish to hear your pleadings and to cure your ills and your sorrow.

As directed, Juan took the message to the bishop of Mexico, Fray Zumarraga, who with the priests were skeptical and sent Juan Diego away. Again the Blessed Virgin appeared to Juan Diego and urged him to return to the bishop to plead her cause. Juan obeyed Our Lady's wish, and this time the bishop asked Juan to return to him with a sign to prove the authenticity of his message.

Three days after the first apparition, the Blessed Virgin appeared again to Juan Diego. To give a sign of proof for the bishop, Our Lady asked Juan to pick the roses that were blooming on Tepeyac Hill, place them in his *tilma,* or cloak, and present them to the bishop. (Since it was the middle of December, the roses were blooming out of season). Bishop Fray Zumarraga was seated as Juan Diego entered the room. Juan spread out his cloak at the bishop's feet, and as the bishop watched the roses cascade to the floor his eyes were drawn to Juan Diego's cloak. The bishop fell from his chair in an act of humility and dropped to his knees, whispering, "It is Mary Immaculate, the Immaculate Conception."

PRAYER TO OUR LADY OF GUADALUPE

Our Lady of Guadalupe, mystical rose, make intercession for the holy Church, protect the Sovereign Pontiff, help all those who invoke you in their necessities, and since you are the ever Virgin Mary and mother of the true God, obtain for us from your most holy Son the grace of keeping our faith, sweet hope in the bitterness of life, burning charity, and the precious gift of final perseverance. Amen.

ABOUT THE SHRINE

The chapel to the left of the sanctuary in St. Mary's Church is both the Chapel of the Most Blessed Sacrament and the Diocesan Shrine of

Our Lady of Guadalupe. The mosaic of Our Lady of Guadalupe tells the story of the apparition of the Virgin Mary to Juan Diego, a Native American Indian, near the town of Guadalupe from what is now the country of Mexico. The mosaic as well as all of the glass etchings in the church were designed by the famous artist Duncan Niles Terry of Rosemont, Pennsylvania. After being designed, the mosaic was then actualized by Farrari and Bucci of Rome, Italy. More than one hundred thousand pieces of Venetian *Smalti* tile were used in this work of art. When the finished mosaic arrived from Rome, it came in 352 segments, which had to be fitted together like a giant jigsaw puzzle. The mosaic is 19 feet tall at its lowest point and 22 feet tall at its highest point, while spanning 20 feet across to cover an area of approximately 410 square feet.

SHRINE INFORMATION

Saint Mary, Our Lady of Guadalupe Church and Shrine
101 West High Street
Kittanning, PA 16201
(724) 548-7649

TOURIST INFORMATION

The Kittanning area has a selection of modern motels to choose from. The Comfort Inn can be found at the intersection of US 422 and 268, and the Quality Inn Royale at 405 Butler Road.

DIRECTIONS TO THE SHRINE

The Shrine of Saint Mary, Our Lady of Guadalupe is about twenty-five miles northeast of Pittsburgh and is easily reached by car. Traveling from the east or west on I-80, take the exit for Rte. 28 south or Rte. 66 south, and follow these roads to Kittanning. For those traveling from the south through Pittsburgh, take Rte. 28 north to Rte. 422 east. The shrine is located approximately six blocks north of Market Street, to the east of the Allegheny River, lock number seven.

FOR FIRST-TIME PILGRIMS

Visitors to the Shrine of Saint Mary, Our Lady of Guadalupe can "read" the story of the apparitions through the mosaic. In addition, pilgrims can trace the history of the Catholic Church in this area by gazing at the chapel windows, although the story is not arranged in chronological order.

OF SPECIAL INTEREST

Why did the parish community in Kittanning choose to name their church building in honor of Saint Mary, Our Lady of Guadalupe? Fr. Francis X. Foley, when preparing the parish community to build their new church building, spoke of how Our Lady of Guadalupe favored a lowly Indian of Aztec descent from an obscure little village with her presence. By her outreach to this one man, she was reaching out to all of us, confirming once again that it is the "poor in spirit" who will win her special friendship and that of her Son. What better place for a lasting shrine to Our Lady than Kittanning, originally a tiny Indian settlement of no major significance, yet rich in its simplicity and in its faith?

Southeast Region

Cathedral Basilica of the Assumption

COVINGTON, KENTUCKY

Built in 1834, St. Mary's Church, Covington's first Catholic Church, served a congregation of both English-speaking and German-speaking Catholics in a small secluded community nestled along the shores of the Ohio River. As Covington's population expanded and its economy flourished, it became necessary to construct a much larger facility, and in 1894 construction began on the new cathedral. The Cathedral Basilica of the Assumption was designed in imitation of the thirteenth-century Gothic style of architecture, conceived in the burgeoning cities around Paris, France. It was dedicated to the Blessed Virgin Mary, celebrating the human vessel by which Christ became man. It was built by the skills of local artisans and craftsmen and funded by the donations of the faithful—a concrete expression of the faith of the community.

This majestic window, the largest church stained-glass window in the world, presents the early fifth-century Ecumenical Council of Ephesus that proclaimed Mary as the Mother of God.
(Cathedral Basilica of the Assumption)

PRAYER TO THE HOLY TRINITY

Let us offer praise and thanksgiving to the Most Holy Trinity, who has shown us the Virgin Mary, clothed with the sun, the moon beneath her feet, and on her head a mystic crown of twelve stars. Let us praise and thank the Divine Father, who elected her

for his daughter. Let us praise and thank the Divine Son, who
became incarnate in her womb. Let us praise the Holy Spirit, by
whose power she was the living temple of the ever-blessed Trin-
ity. Amen.

ABOUT THE SHRINE

The Marian shrine, which flanks the main altar in the cathedral, was designed by August Schmidt, carved by him in his native Cologne, Germany, and installed in 1957. Frieze carvings of lindenwood in the massive oak frame of the shrine trace the seven joys and seven sorrows of the Blessed Mother of Jesus. The fine features of the white Carrara marble sculpture of Mary can be appreciated in its elaborate surroundings. The Marian prayer at the left, along with its calligraphy and illumination, is the work of Sister Bernetta, S.C.N., a local artist.

The stained-glass windows in the cathedral are art treasures made in Munich, Germany. The majestic north transept window, sixty-seven feet in length by twenty-four feet in width, is the largest church stained-glass window in the world. It presents the early fifth-century Ecumenical Council of Ephesus that proclaimed Mary as the Mother of God. Its upper tier illustrates the coronation of Mary as Queen of Heaven and Earth, and its lower tier illustrates the saints of noted devotion to the Blessed Virgin.

SHRINE INFORMATION

Cathedral Basilica of the Assumption
1140 Madison Avenue
Covington, KY 41011
(606) 431-2060
fax: (606) 431-8444

TOURIST INFORMATION

Specific restaurant and hotel accommodations in the immediate area can be obtained by writing to the above address.

DIRECTIONS TO THE SHRINE

Covington, Kentucky, is just across the Ohio River from Cincinnati, Ohio. Take I-75 south to 12th Street. Go east on 12th Street to Madison Avenue. The cathedral and rectory are on the corner. Parking lots are available behind the cathedral on the north side and across Madison Avenue in front of the cathedral.

FOR FIRST-TIME PILGRIMS

The cathedral is open daily from 10:00 A.M. through 4:00 P.M., except on holy days and holidays. Volunteers are on hand to welcome pilgrims. The gift shop and museum, located in the rectory, are open Tuesday through Saturday from 10:00 A.M. through 4:00 P.M. and Sunday from 11:00 A.M. through 4:00 P.M., except on holy days and holidays. To learn more about the history and art of the cathedral, pilgrims are invited to take the guided tour available on Sunday at 11:00 A.M. after the morning Mass. For more information or to arrange a guided tour for your group during the week, call the Cathedral Business Office at (606) 431-2060 to schedule an appointment.

Mass is celebrated daily at 10:00 A.M., on Saturday at 4:30 P.M., and on Sunday at 10:00 A.M. and 5:30 P.M.

OF SPECIAL INTEREST

A visit to the Cathedral Basilica of the Assumption is like stepping back into another time, another place. Begun in 1894, the cathedral, with an exterior patterned after that of Notre Dame in Paris, is a work in progress. Housed within this glorious edifice is an impressive collection of religious art and artifacts, including beautifully detailed Italian mosaics, murals by world-renowned artist Frank Duveneck, the largest hand-blown church stained-glass window in the world, historic organs, and intricate wood carvings. Sitting on lofty perches against the backdrop of the Cincinnati skyline, gargoyles have stood guard for generations over this magnificent example of Gothic architecture in the United States.

+‖+
+‖+

Catholic Shrine
of the Immaculate Conception

ATLANTA, GEORGIA

When the city of Atlanta was founded in 1837, it was called Terminus because it was the end of the railroad line. Many of the railroad workers were Irish Catholics, and so the Church of the Immaculate Conception began. A wooden structure was erected in 1848 on the present site of the shrine under the guidance of an Irish missionary, Fr. John Barry.

The Irish connection continued for decades. It was Fr. Thomas O'Reilly, a native Irishman and Confederate chaplain, who persuaded Gen. William Tecumseh Sherman to spare his church and that of his neighbors. Legend has it that Father O'Reilly told Sherman, "If you burn the Catholic church, all Catholics in the ranks of the Union Army will mutiny."

The cornerstone of the present structure was laid in 1869, and the structure was completed and dedicated in 1873. Father O'Reilly died in 1872 and was buried in a crypt under the main altar.

The shrine had to be rebuilt in 1982 following a disastrous fire. At that time, two caskets were uncovered in an area previously considered a storeroom. These hold the remains of Father O'Reilly and Fr. Thomas Francis Cleary. The latter, a native of Georgia, was educated in Ireland and served as pastor of Immaculate Conception from 1881 to 1884. The crypt was restored and opened to the public in 1988. This area, in the basement of the shrine, is open for guided tours.

PRAYER TO THE BLESSED VIRGIN

O pure and immaculate and likewise Blessed Virgin, you who are the sinless Mother of your Son, the mighty Lord of the universe, you who are inviolate and altogether holy, the hope of the hopeless and sinful, we sing your praises. We bless you, as full of every grace, you who bore the God-Man: we all bow low before you; we invoke you and implore your aid. Rescue us, O holy and inviolate Virgin, from every necessity that presses upon us and from all the temptations of the devil. Be our intercession and advocate at the hour of our death and judgment; deliver us from the fire that is not extinguished and from the outer darkness; make us worthy of the glory of your Son, O dearest and most clement Virgin Mother. You indeed are our only hope most sure and sacred in God's sight, to whom be honor and glory, majesty and dominion, for ever and ever, world without end. Amen.

ABOUT THE SHRINE

In the sanctuary, twelve ornate chandeliers softly highlight the ceiling, with its paintings of the Twelve Apostles by Georgian artist Henry Barnes, and the stained-glass aisle windows, with their religious symbols. The main altar of the church was restored after the fire of 1982. Both side altars survived intact. The statue of the Pietà, carved in Italy, also survived the fire and stands in its original place. A Moller pipe organ designed specifically to meet the needs of the acoustics and the depth of the church is considered outstanding by both national and local artists.

In addition to the shrine's liturgies and scheduled tours, the shrine is open to visitors during the day through specially designed doors. These doors were installed through the effort of the Friends of the Shrine. Founded in 1988, this organization is dedicated to preserving the shrine, the oldest symbol of Catholicism in Atlanta.

The carillon and the outside lighting add to the beauty of the entire edifice. The carillon can be heard daily at noon and again at 6:00 P.M. when the Angelus is rung. Guests interested in architectural beauty may find it worthwhile to return to the area after dark to see the outside lighting, another gift of the Friends of the Shrine.

SHRINE INFORMATION

The Catholic Shrine of the Immaculate Conception
48 Martin Luther King, Jr., Drive SW
Atlanta, GA 30303
(404) 521-1866
website: http://www.catholicshrineatlanta.org

TOURIST INFORMATION

Located at the corner of Central Avenue and Martin Luther King, Jr., Drive, the Catholic Shrine of the Immaculate Conception is an architectural landmark. The shrine is also Atlanta's oldest Catholic church. It shares a city block with Central Presbyterian Church. Trinity United Methodist Church is nearby. Business, entertainment, industry, government, and Georgia State University are all within easy walking distance of the shrine, which is across the street from the World of Coca-Cola and Underground Atlanta.

Restaurant and hotel accommodations are easily accessible in the immediate area.

DIRECTIONS TO THE SHRINE

The shrine is located at the corner of Central Avenue, across from the Coke Museum and Underground Atlanta. Disabled access is available from Martin Luther King, Jr., Drive at the rear of the church.

FOR FIRST-TIME PILGRIMS

The Shrine of the Immaculate Conception is open for tours from June 1 to September 28 on Sundays only from 1:00 to 4:00 P.M. Mass is celebrated on weekdays at 12:10 P.M., on Saturday at 9:00 A.M., and on Sunday at 8:30 and 11:30 A.M.

OF SPECIAL INTEREST

Throughout its history, the parishioners of the shrine have been dedicated to community service, from ministering to Confederate soldiers during the Civil War, to the current establishment of a night shelter during the winter months. St. Francis Table feeds the hungry on Saturday mornings, and the church is involved in many AIDS ministries.

Grotto and Pilgrimage Shrine of Our Lady of Lourdes

BELMONT ABBEY
BELMONT, NORTH CAROLINA

In 1891 Fr. Francis Meyer, O.S.B., a monk of the abbey at Belmont, fell prey to typhoid fever. He was near death when Fr. Felix Hintemeyer, O.S.B., prior of the monastery, placed Father Francis' health in the special care of Our Lady, promising to build a grotto in her honor (under the title of Lourdes) if Father Francis lived. Father Francis was out of bed the next morning, and he lived for another fourteen years. In response, the brothers of the monastery immediately set to building the grotto under Father Felix's direction. Its design was modeled after the cove at Lourdes. America's abbot-bishop, Leo M. Haid, O.S.B. (who was then abbot-ordinary of Belmont Abbey and bishop of the Vicariate Apostolic of North Carolina), decided to bless the grotto as a pilgrimage shrine, naming it a center of prayers for priestly vocations. Fr. Francis Meyer, his health restored, was at the bishop's side during the blessing.

An artist, Hans Kelly Somey, restored the statues of the shrine in 1993, when the site was placed on the National Register of Historic Places as part of the Belmont Abbey Historic District.

PRAYER TO MARY

Holy Mary, be a help to the helpless, strength to the fearful, comfort to the sorrowful; pray for the people, plead for the clergy, intercede for all holy women consecrated to God; may all who keep the sacred memory experience the power of your assistance. Amen.

ABOUT THE SHRINE

In 1891 the Grotto and Pilgrimage Shrine of Maria Lourdes was constructed and devotional use initiated. In 1895 the Holy See gave the

Each evening in May, the monks process to the Grotto and Pilgrimage Shrine of Our Lady of Lourdes after vespers for the Litany of Loreto, the Memorare, and the Marian Antiphon. *(Archives of Belmont Abbey, Belmont, NC)*

Benedictines in North Carolina the privilege of celebrating the Feast of Our Lady of Lourdes. To this day, each evening in May, the monks process to the shrine after vespers for the Litany of Loreto, the Memorare, and the Marian Antiphon. The shrine is open year-round and has also been the site of religious professions, Mothers' Day observances, weddings, and other celebrations. Special pilgrimages have been arranged during Marian and Holy Years and other important occasions. At present, a group of laity, on their own initiative, visit the abbey each first Saturday through the year.

SHRINE INFORMATION

Belmont Abbey
100 Belmont-Mount Holly Road
Belmont, NC 28012-1802
Contact: Dom Paschal Baumstein, O.S.B., Abbey Historian, (704) 825-6775 for historical information, or Reverend Guestmaster, (704) 825-6564, for information about visiting the abbey and shrine.

TOURIST INFORMATION

Belmont Abbey does not have a guesthouse, but there are various hotels in the area. Further information can be obtained by writing to

Gaston County Office of Tourism
212 West Main Avenue
P.O. Box 1578
Gastonia, NC 28053

DIRECTIONS TO THE SHRINE

The abbey is located about ten miles west of downtown Charlotte. If driving from Charlotte, take I-85 south toward Gastonia. Belmont is the first town after Charlotte. Use the Belmont Abbey College exit. At the end of the exit, go left; the first right thereafter is the main entrance to Belmont Abbey College. The Abbey Church is clearly visible as you enter. Parking is available nearby. In the vestibule of the church are brochures about the grotto, with directions for walking there (about three minutes by foot). No public transportation other than taxis serves the abbey.

FOR FIRST-TIME PILGRIMS

Visitors are welcome to the grotto throughout the year, but the monastery itself is not open to the public. The abbey grounds are well kept and are especially beautiful in spring and summer. Pilgrims appreciate and respect the quiet of the grotto, which is an ideal site for private meditation and pilgrimage. The monks' celebrations of the Divine Office and Mass in the Abbey Church are open to the public. Confession is available before Mass or by appointment. If visitors attend vespers in May, they are welcome to join the monks in processing to the grotto afterward for devotions.

Lavatories are available in nearby buildings, and a number of off-campus eating establishments are located conveniently near the campus. Handicapped access to the grotto is complicated by stairs, and some ground coverings of stone and gravel make wheelchair maneuvering difficult.

OF SPECIAL INTEREST

In the college bookstore, two relevant publications are on sale. The first, a biography of the Benedictine life in North Carolina, is titled *My Lord of Belmont* and includes the story of the grotto and shrine. The second publication, *Blessing the Years to Come,* is a photographic history of the campus, including the grotto and shrine.

Mary, Queen of the Universe

ORLANDO, FLORIDA

Mary, Queen of the Universe Shrine is truly a house built upon faith. Beginning years ago, Mass was celebrated as a tourist ministry for visitors to Central Florida, with folding chairs and makeshift altars set up in hotel meeting rooms. As the numbers of visitors climbed, the need to build a home away from home for the faithful became evident—a place that would welcome all and proclaim to each the gospel message and the maternal love of Mary, Mother of God. Encouraged by His Holiness Pope John Paul II, energized by a resurgent devotion to Our Lady,

Mary, Queen of the Universe was constructed stone-by-stone through the prayerful offerings of visitors to Florida from around the world. *(Mary, Queen of the Universe)*

and endowed with the prayerful offerings of brothers and sisters in Christ, the shrine was built—with every brick and tile, each wooden pew, and every pane of glass inscribed with faith. From this place, the faithful have carried away a renewed sense of God's presence in their lives; and here they have left something of themselves—a sacrifice that will help light the path to Christ for the generations yet ahead.

PRAYER TO MARY, QUEEN OF THE UNIVERSE

Majestic Queen of Heaven and Mistress of the Angels, you received from God the power and commission to crush the head of Satan; we beseech you, send forth the legions of heaven, that under your command they may seek out all evil spirits, engage them everywhere in battle, curb their insolence, and hurl them back into the pit of hell. O good and tender Mother, be our hope and our object of love. Holy angels and archangels, defend us and keep us. Amen.

ABOUT THE SHRINE

More than twenty-two million people visit Orlando each year, coming from every state and from around the world. Some five million of these annual visitors are Catholic. Hence the need for an appropriate—and unifying—place of worship. And no place could be more appropriately unifying than a shrine dedicated in the name of Mary, Queen of the Universe.

Constructed stone-by-stone through the prayerful offerings of men, women, and children from around the world, and declared by Pope John Paul II as a "house of pilgrimage," Mary, Queen of the Universe Shrine was dedicated on August 22, 1993. Among the last great shrines of the second millennium, it is today a place of welcome for all peoples, providing a richly spiritual experience. The facilities include

- a two-thousand-seat Marian church
- the Magnificat Windows (fourteen stained-glass windows)
- the Chapel of Our Lady of Guadalupe
- counseling and confession sessions
- an outdoor Mother and Child Chapel
- Stations of the Cross by Franz Ansele
- a religious gifts and book shop
- Rosary Garden
- the Blessed Sacrament Chapel for Perpetual Adoration

SHRINE INFORMATION

Mary, Queen of the Universe Shrine
8300 Vineland Avenue
Orlando, FL 32821
(407) 239-6600
fax: (407) 239-1362
e-mail: maryqu@ix.netcom.com

TOURIST INFORMATION

There are many hotels in the area of Lake Buena Vista on Hotel Boulevard and also on International Drive. None are within walking distance of the shrine, but many are about five or ten minutes by car. The shrine is very near Walt Disney World and Sea World and about ten minutes' drive from Universal Studios.

DIRECTIONS TO THE SHRINE

FROM ORLANDO

Take I-4 west to exit 27 (Lake Buena Vista). Turn left on S.R. 535, stay in the left lane, and turn left at the light onto Vineland Avenue (at Little Lake Bryan), just before the Holiday Inn.

FROM TAMPA

Take I-4 north to exit 27 (Lake Buena Vista). Drive straight to the shrine (no turns).

FROM LAKE BUENA VISTA HOTELS

Take S.R. 535 south (toward I-4), go under I-4, and continue in the left lane to Vineland Avenue (about three hundred yards). Turn left at the traffic light on Vineland Avenue (at Little Lake Bryan) and proceed to the shrine entrance.

FROM THE INTERNATIONAL DRIVE AREA AND SOUTHWEST AREA

Follow International Drive south to Little Lake Bryan Parkway (1.1 miles south of the Mission Club). Turn right, then right again, and follow the parkway to the shrine.

FOR COMMERCIAL TRANSPORTATION

Inquire at the hotel/motel desk, or call 828-3036.

FOR FIRST-TIME PILGRIMS

Mary, Queen of the Universe Shrine is open daily from 7:30 A.M. through 5:00 P.M. Mass is celebrated daily at 8:00 A.M., on Saturday at 6:00 P.M., and on Sunday and holy days at 7:30, 9:30, and 11:30 A.M. and

6:00 P.M. Mass and the perpetual novena of the Miraculous Medal are celebrated every Monday evening at 7:00 P.M.

First-time visitors to the shrine will enjoy the walking tour utilizing headsets available at the gift shop. There is no charge for using the headsets, and the tour, which lasts about one hour, begins on the bridge leading to the shrine and includes the Rosary Garden as well as the main church and all of the artwork.

Some special events at the shrine include the Mother's Day novena in May, when roses are placed on the altar (ten thousand roses in 1997!); the Annual Rosary Walk in October; a life-size Nativity display in November and December; and the Stations of the Cross during Lent.

OF SPECIAL INTEREST

There are several opportunities for creating memorials at the shrine, whether it be a tree in the Rosary Garden or a plaque in the Mother and Child Outdoor Chapel. The shrine has no local parish family and is funded entirely by donations from tourists visiting the Central Florida area from all corners of this country and from most other countries as well.

National Shrine of Our Lady of Prompt Succor
URSULINE CONVENT
NEW ORLEANS, LOUISIANA

On February 22, 1727, a band of French Ursulines set sail on the *Gironde* from Lorient, a port in Brittany, and reached the city of New Orleans on the morning of August 7 of the same year. Shortly after their arrival, the nuns began their work of teaching the children of the colonists and nursing the sick in the hospital placed under their care. They opened in October 1727 the Catholic school that has the longest continuous history in the United States.

The statue of Our Lady of Prompt Succor, now venerated by

Our Lady of Prompt Succor is honored with an annual Mass of Thanksgiving for Gen. Andrew Jackson's victory over British forces at the Battle of New Orleans during the War of 1812. *(National Shrine of Our Lady of Prompt Succor)*

Orleanians for over 150 years, arrived from France in the year 1810. Mother St. Michael Gensoul brought the statue to Louisiana from her native land and solemnly installed it in the Ursuline Convent Chapel in fulfillment of a promise to have Mary "honored in New Orleans under the title of Our Lady of Prompt Succor."

On January 7, 1815, the British Army under the command of Sir Edward Pakenham was preparing for its attack the next morning against the greatly outnumbered forces of Gen. Andrew Jackson. Throughout the night the mothers, wives, and loved ones of the men on the American side of the Chalmette battlefield kept a vigil of prayer before the statue of Our Lady of Prompt Succor in the Ursuline chapel on Chartres Street. The following morning, Fr. William Bubourg offered a Mass to "the God of Battles," and the Ursulines through their superior, Mother Marie Olivier de Vezin, made the vow to have a Mass of Thanksgiving sung annually should the Americans be victorious. At the moment of Communion a messenger rushed into the chapel announcing the glad tidings of the enemy's defeat. Ever since this memorable day in 1815, the Ursulines have kept their vow.

PRAYER TO OUR LADY OF PROMPT SUCCOR

Our Lady of Prompt Succor, ever Virgin Mother of Jesus Christ our Lord and God, you are most powerful against the enemy of our salvation. The divine promise of a redeemer was announced right after the sin of our first parents; and you, through your Divine Son, crushed the serpent's head. Hasten, then, to our help and deliver us from the deceits of Satan. Intercede for us with Jesus that we may always accept God's graces and be found faithful

to him in our particular states of life. As you once saved our be-
loved city from ravaging flames and our country from an in-
vading army, have pity on us and obtain for us protection from
hurricanes and all other disasters. (Silent pause for individual
petitions.) Assist us in the many trials that beset our path through
life. Watch over the Church and the pope as they uphold with
total fidelity the purity of faith and morals against unremitting
opposition. Be to us truly Our Lady of Prompt Succor now and
especially at the hour of our death, that we may gain everlasting
life through the merits of Jesus Christ who lives and reigns with
the Father and the Holy Spirit, one God, world without end.
Amen.

ABOUT THE SHRINE

At the time the National Shrine of Our Lady of Prompt Succor was built, the Ursuline Sisters were still semicloistered. This is the reason for the L-shaped building: two chapels facing the same sanctuary. The Sisters used the inside chapel, and the public the outside chapel. A grill separated the sanctuary from the inside chapel. This was removed in 1965 as a result of changes set in motion by Pope John XXIII and Vatican II.

The outside chapel dedicated to the Blessed Virgin Mary is known as the National Shrine of Our Lady of Prompt Succor. It was dedicated on January 8, 1924, and consecrated on January 6, 1928. This is a double chapel attached to the convent and school, which was erected in 1912. The shrine was made an historic landmark during the bicentennial year of our country because it housed the then 166-year-old statue of Our Lady. Outside the main entrance of the chapel is a statue of Our Lady with the inscription in Latin "To Mary the Victorious"—an allusion to the victory reported by Andrew Jackson on January 8, 1815, on the battlefield of Chalmette.

SHRINE INFORMATION

National Shrine of Our Lady of Prompt Succor
Ursuline Convent
Archives and Museum
2635 State Street
New Orleans, LA 70118

TOURIST INFORMATION

Specific information regarding restaurants and overnight accommodations can be obtained by writing to the above address.

DIRECTIONS TO THE SHRINE

The shrine is located on State Street within a reasonable distance to the Uptown Square Shopping Center and the Memorial Medical Center of New Orleans. Not far away is Notre Dame Seminary, Xavier University, and the Carrolton Cemetery. For visitors to New Orleans, a map of the city is essential and a worthwhile investment, and with these landmarks noted, your most direct route to the shrine will be easily discovered.

OF SPECIAL INTEREST

The annals of the Ursulines report that General Jackson went in person to the convent to thank the nuns for their prayers. According to the Ursulines, this was the second time that Our Lady of Prompt Succor had interceded for New Orleans. In 1812, when a fire was ravaging the city, and the wind was driving the flames toward the Ursuline convent and the nearby buildings, one of the Sisters, before fleeing from the cloister, placed a small statue of Our Lady of Prompt Succor on a windowsill facing the fire. At the same time, another Sister prayed aloud, "Our Lady of Prompt Succor, hasten to our help or we are lost." Scarcely had she uttered the last word when the wind changed direction and the convent and environs were saved. Witnesses attested to this fact.

Our Lady of the Angels Monastery
SHRINE OF THE BLESSED SACRAMENT
BIRMINGHAM, ALABAMA

For most of us, life in today's hurried world can be summarized in one word: whirlwind. We're blown by the winds of time from project to project or crisis to crisis. Often, living our faith gets lost in the gusts of activity. To calm the storm, we attempt to set aside a holy hour. But after fifteen minutes, we're either asleep or consumed by distractions. Frustrated, we quit.

Jesus commanded his disciples to "come away by yourselves to a quiet place, and rest awhile." More than anyone else, he understood their need

The chapel at Our Lady of the Angels Monastery offers pilgrims the opportunity to bow down in worship before the Presence of the Lord. *(Our Lady of the Angels Monastery)*

to rest and be alone with him. That need is perhaps even greater for followers today. All of us must intentionally seek time to reflect prayerfully upon our lives and to make a commitment to Jesus. Where better to make such a commitment than in the presence of the Eucharist? Pilgrimages to Our Lady of the Angels Monastery and Shrine of the Blessed Sacrament offer the perfect opportunity for prayer, reflection, and renewal.

PRAYER TO OUR LADY OF THE BLESSED SACRAMENT

O Virgin Mary, our Lady of the Blessed Sacrament, glory of the Christian people, joy of the universal Church, salvation of the whole world, pray for us, and awaken in all believers a lively devotion toward the most holy Eucharist, so that we may be made worthy to receive this most precious gift daily for our nourishment and our strength. Amen.

ABOUT THE SHRINE

A sense of holiness will overwhelm you as you pass through the gates of Our Lady of the Angels Monastery. Entering the chapel, you are at once awed by the Blessed Sacrament, exposed for veneration in an exquisite silver and gold monstrance. Here, in a quiet retreat from the world, you can bow down in worship before the Presence of the Lord. Or you may also walk the Stations of the Cross, seek out the outdoor chapel, and enjoy any of the peaceful garden spots for prayer.

SHRINE INFORMATION

Julia Tucker, Director of Pilgrimages
5817 Old Leeds Road
Birmingham, AL 35210
(205) 271-2966
fax: (205) 271-2957

TOURIST INFORMATION

Pilgrimages to Our Lady of the Angels Monastery and Shrine of the Blessed Sacrament are designed for groups of ten or more. Special group rates have been coordinated with local hotels, and box lunches can be arranged upon request. For groups flying into Birmingham, all hotels have courtesy buses that will pick you up from the airport. All travel to Birmingham will be arranged by a group organizer. The only expenses involved are for travel, accommodations, and meals.

DIRECTIONS TO THE SHRINE

For pilgrims traveling by car, the monastery and shrine can best be reached by proceeding south on I-20 from Birmingham, or north on I-20 from Atlanta. The exit is 133, Kilgore Memorial Road, east to Old Leeds Road. For those coming from Tuscaloosa and the west, the exit is number 27, Grant Mills Road. Proceed northwest on Grant Mills Road to Old Leeds Road, and then go left on Old Leeds Road.

FOR FIRST-TIME PILGRIMS

Time spent in the presence of God is not easily forgotten. As one pilgrim wrote, "It was like a foretaste of heaven." No wonder so many feel that the Our Lady of the Angels Monastery and Shrine of the Blessed Sacrament is a special place. The shrine is open for prayer from 6:00 A.M. until 6:00 P.M. Mass is celebrated every morning at 7:00 A.M. with the nuns who are members of the monastery community. Out of respect for Jesus' presence in the Blessed Sacrament, pilgrims are asked not to wear shorts, tank tops, or miniskirts in the chapel.

Retreats are arranged for groups of ten or more. Individual pilgrims are welcome to join in with any group that is on retreat, or they are welcome to make their own private retreat. The retreat experience revolves around a schedule of Mass, the rosary, confession, a healing service, guided tours, and spiritual talks.

The grounds of the Shrine of the Blessed Sacrament are full of constant reminders of God's beauty. The Stations of the Cross, Shrine of the Unborn, and Pietà are located on the grounds for personal meditation while on retreat. Also located on the grounds are two outdoor altars for special feast-day celebrations.

OF SPECIAL INTEREST

This holy place is the home of EWTN, the Catholic global communications network. The mission of EWTN and the vision that is provided by Mother Angelica are central to the monastery and shrine. Daily Mass is broadcast live on EWTN at 7:00 A.M. and again at noon. *Pillars of Faith* with Bishop Foley is open to the public each Monday night at 7:00 P.M. Central time. *Mother Angelica Live* is also open to the public every Tuesday and Wednesday night at 7:00 P.M. Pilgrims are asked to arrive by 6:30 P.M. so that everyone can be seated before airtime. Tours of the EWTN studio are available in accessible areas; however, when a program is taping, access to the studio is limited to scheduled breaks.

Shrine of Our Lady of La Leche
MISSION OF NOMBRE DE DIOS
ST. AUGUSTINE, FLORIDA

In 1565 Spanish explorers established the first permanent community of settlers, in what was to become the United States, in St. Augustine. It was here that Fr. Francisco López de Mendoza Grajales offered the first Mass in the New World. On the grounds of the Mission of Nombre de Dios—the Name of God—the early Spanish settlers established the first shrine ever to be dedicated to the Blessed Virgin Mary in the United States.

The original chapel, built around 1615, was ruined in the early eighteenth century during an attack on St. Augustine. Once rebuilt, the

The Shrine of Our Lady of La Leche enshrines a replica of the original statue of Nuestra Señora de la Leche y buen parto— Our Lady of the Mild and Happy Delivery. *(Shrine of Our Lady of La Leche)*

chapel was destroyed by a hurricane. In 1915 the present chapel was built and enshrines a replica of the original statue of Nuestra Señora de la Leche y buen parto—Our Lady of the Mild and Happy Delivery. Throughout its existence, the shrine has remained a comforting place of prayer for mothers-to-be, for families, for those with special intentions, and for those seeking to strengthen their faith.

As you walk through the historic grounds at the mission, you will be retracing the steps of America's first settlers more than four hundred years ago. This is the site where Western culture and Christian faith took root in our country.

PRAYER TO THE MOTHER OF THE SON OF GOD

O Mary, I wonder at that profound humility, which troubled your blessed heart at the message of the Angel Gabriel, that you had been chosen to be the Mother of the Son of the Most High God. I beg of you the grace of a contrite and humble heart, so that, acknowledging my misery, I may come to attain the glory promised to those who are truly humble of heart. Amen.

SHRINE INFORMATION

Eric Johnson, Assistant Director
Mission of Nombre de Dios
30 Ocean Avenue
St. Augustine, FL 32084
(904) 824-3045
fax: (904) 829-0819

TOURIST INFORMATION

No restaurant or overnight accommodations are available at the shrine or the mission; however, contacting the assistant director at the above address will provide you with specific information to make arrangements for your visit.

DIRECTIONS TO THE SHRINE

The Shrine of Our Lady of La Leche is located just a few blocks north of St. Augustine's Tourist Information Center, which is clearly marked. Directions to the mission church and the shrine are easily followed from this central point in the city.

FOR FIRST-TIME PILGRIMS

In addition to the Chapel and Shrine of Our Lady of La Leche, pilgrims may visit the Prince of Peace Church, view the 208-foot stainless-steel cross, the Father López statue, a diorama of the founding of St. Augustine, and the mission plaque. Or for solitude and prayer reflection, pilgrims may tour the beautiful and peaceful grounds of the mission.

OF SPECIAL INTEREST

The Mission of Nombre de Dios, the site of the Shrine of Our Lady of La Leche, is the first permanent Christian settlement in the United States. It was founded by Pedro Menendez de Aviles and his band of settlers in 1565. The Spanish pioneers named this landing site Nombre de Dios—the Name of God—in honor of the Holy Name of Jesus. The founding of the Mission of Nombre de Dios marked the beginning of missionary work in the sixteenth century by Spanish diocesan priests, Jesuits, and Franciscans along the Atlantic coast from present-day Miami to the Chesapeake Bay and westward to Pensacola, Florida.

Southwest Region

+‖+
+‖+

"Lourdes of America"
EL SANTUARIO DE CHIMAYO,
CHIMAYO, NEW MEXICO

If you are a stranger, if you are weary from the struggles in life,
whether you have a handicap, whether you have a broken heart,
follow the long mountain road, find a home in Chimayo....
In all the places in the world that I have been, this must be heaven....
C. MENDOSA, LAS CRUCES, NEW MEXICO

Although it is not a Marian shrine, not even by the wildest stretch of imagination, we could not leave El Santuario out of our book, especially since it is often called the "Lourdes of America" because of the many pilgrims that flock to this site for spiritual and physical help. El Santuario, or as it is officially known "The Shrine of Our Lord of Escuipulas," has a long history. It was built somewhere between 1814 and 1816, the successor to a small private chapel built in 1810 by Don Bernardo Abeyta in order to house the miraculous crucifix of Our Lord of Escuipulas that was in his possession. It was a privately owned chapel until 1929, when it was purchased from the Chavez family and legal title was given to the Archdiocese of Santa Fe, New Mexico.

ABOUT THE SHRINE

More than three hundred thousand pilgrims come to the shrine each year. Pilgrims with a special devotion to the Blessed Mother will find particular points of interest that will make a visit even more memorable.

Chimayo is famous for five *reredos* (a series of sacred paintings) that can be found behind the main altar and to the right and the left of the sanctuary. Immediately to your left the *reredos* painted by José Aragon of Chamisal is of special interest. In the upper row, left to right, you can find Our Lady of Mount Carmel, Mary, the Immaculate Conception, and Our Lady of St. John of the Lakes. In the next *reredos*, by the same artist, you will find in the top row Our Lady of Guadalupe, which is modeled after the painting in the Basilica of Guadalupe in

Mexico City. As you move around the church, you will discover the fifth *reredos,* painted by Molleno. It shows, in the top row, a depiction of Our Lady of Sorrows, with a dagger in her heart.

The sanctuary of Chimayo is also famous for *el pocito,* the little well. In a room just off the main altar and easily discovered, you will find the "holy dirt" that many pilgrims take from this place in the belief that it will be of spiritual benefit to them. Some people eat the dirt, a practice found among Indians of South and Central America and also among some people with iron-poor blood.

SHRINE INFORMATION

Holy Family Church
P.O. Box 235
Chimayo, NM 87522
(505) 351-4889/4360

TOURIST INFORMATION

Restaurants and motel accommodations are readily available within a short driving distance of Chimayo.

DIRECTIONS TO THE SHRINE

Chimayo is about twenty-five miles north of Santa Fe. El Santuario advertises itself as "a stop on the high road to Taos." The best way to travel to Chimayo is by car. Travel north of Sante Fe on State Hwy. 285/84 for approximately eighteen miles to State Road Junction 503, then proceed northeast for approximately eight miles. County Road 98 (formerly State Road

520) will be on your left; turn and follow the county road for approximately three miles. Signs for El Santuario will direct you the rest of the way.

FOR FIRST-TIME PILGRIMS

El Santuario de Chimayo is a place to pray and to meditate. The simplicity of the site is something that most modern people need a little time to adjust to. It is well worth the effort to do just that. Don't rush through your visit. Take time to appreciate the *reredos,* explore the *bultos* (carvings), and take special notice of "El Señor Santiago," a man on horseback, representing Saint James. Finally, visit the gift shop, since all proceeds from the shop are used for the support of the church.

Visiting hours are 9:00 A.M. through 4:00 P.M. October–April, and 9:00 A.M. through 6:00 P.M. May–September. Weekly Mass May–September is at 11:00 A.M., and during the months of October–April Mass is celebrated at 7:00 A.M. Sunday Mass is celebrated at noon throughout the year.

OF SPECIAL INTEREST

About one block northwest of El Santuario, just beyond the El Portrero Plaza, you can discover the Chapel of El Santo Niño de Atocha (Chapel of the Holy Child). It is at this chapel that the practice of offering baby shoes, a practice that seems to be unique to northern New Mexico, takes place. According to legend, El Santo Niño leaves the chapel at night and walks around the country, healing sick children. The Holy Child wears out his shoes in performing this mission and needs new shoes in order to continue. This beautiful story is an example of the deep faith that is found in the people of a certain time and place, a faith still found today among the people who continue to pray to Jesus under the title of El Santo Niño de Atocha.

$$\boxed{+\!+}\atop\boxed{+\!+}$$

Our Lady of Czestochowa Shrine

SERAPHIC SISTERS OF OUR LADY OF SORROWS
SAN ANTONIO, TEXAS

My special place is Our Lady of Czestochowa (at Beethoven Street and Rigsby Ave.) where there is peace and quiet and solace. You can come out of there filled with your prayers. It is a small shrine built by Polish people.
SAN ANTONIO EXPRESS-NEWS, AUGUST 26, 1995

The Grotto and Shrine of Our Lady of Czestochowa was built in 1966 to commemorate Poland's one thousand years of embracing Christianity, from 966 to 1966. This grotto is also a memorial to American soldiers who served in both World Wars, the Korean War, and the Vietnam War and gave their lives for the freedom of our country. This grotto is known as the Peace Grotto, and prayers said here are offered for peace.

PRAYER TO THE VIRGIN OF VIRGINS

Remember, O most gracious Virgin Mary, that never was it known that anyone who fled to thy protection, implored thy help, or sought thy intercession, was left unaided. Inspired by this confidence, I fly unto thee, O Virgin of virgins, my Mother. To thee do I come, before thee I stand, sinful and sorrowful. O Mother of the Word Incarnate! Despise not my petitions, but in thy mercy, hear and answer me. Amen.

ABOUT THE SHRINE

Although a new chapel for the shrine is currently under construction, the old chapel remains and will house the picture of Our Lady of Czestochowa, or the "Black Madonna," considered one of the most famous and most miraculous pictures in the world today. Many miracle stories of Mary's intervention and many private cures of pilgrims are attributed to this picture. In one celebrated story in the seventeenth century, Poland came under attack by the Swedes. A group of monks and knights, under the command of the Pauline prior Kordecki, repulsed the repeated attacks of the Swedes and credited their victory to the direct intervention of the Mother of God.

The grotto stands over thirty feet high and is believed to be the largest grotto in the world. Also on the grounds is a museum with memorabilia pertaining to the Polish culture and witnessing to the attachment of the Polish people to the Blessed Mother.

Our Lady of Czestochowa, the "Black Madonna," is considered one of the most famous and most miraculous pictures in the world today. *(Our Lady of Czestochowa Shrine)*

SHRINE INFORMATION

Seraphic Sisters of Our Lady of Sorrows
130 Beethoven Street
San Antonio, TX 78210
(210) 337-8193 or (210) 333-4582

TOURIST INFORMATION

There are no restaurant or hotel accommodations at the shrine at present, but many facilities are available quite close to the shrine.

DIRECTIONS TO THE SHRINE

Our Lady of Czestochowa Shrine is located in the southeastern portion of San Antonio, not too far from Southside Lions Park.

FROM THE SAN ANTONIO AIRPORT

Take I-37 (Rte. 281) south and exit onto I-10 east, then exit on Roland. Turn right onto Roland and right again on Aurelia Street. Go to the end of Aurelia and turn right on Rigsby. Turn left on the first street, which is Beethoven Street, and on the left side you will almost immediately see the grounds. The drive from the airport to the shrine takes about twenty minutes.

FOR FIRST-TIME PILGRIMS

Devotions are conducted at the Shrine of Our Lady of Czestochowa throughout the year. Daily Mass is celebrated at 9:00 A.M. and on Sundays at 10:00 A.M. Adoration of the Blessed Sacrament continues daily until 5:00 P.M. An all-night vigil, beginning with holy Mass at 8:30 P.M. and ending with a Eucharistic celebration at 6:00 A.M., is held every first Friday. On Tuesdays, the novena to the Blessed Mother of Perpetual Help is recited before the morning Masses.

The Way of the Cross is conducted each Friday at 5:00 P.M. during Lent. An artist from Poland has erected the fourteen Stations of the Cross in the form of wayside chapels.

OF SPECIAL INTEREST

In the famous picture of Our Lady of Czestochowa, or the Black Madonna, the Mother and Child are black. Some say this is the result of smoke damage that occurred during a fire at the shrine in Poland many years ago. Still others believe that the smoke rising from the many candles that were lighted and burned in front of the picture for hundreds of years darkened the faces of the Mother and Child. Perhaps it has something to do with a Bible verse in the Song of Songs, "I am black but beautiful," and was originally painted that way. Who knows?

West Region

✠

The Grotto—National Sanctuary of Our Sorrowful Mother

ORDER OF SERVANTS OF MARY
PORTLAND, OREGON

Fr. Ambrose M. Mayer, O.S.M., founded the National Sanctuary of Our Sorrowful Mother, popularly known as The Grotto, in 1923 in fulfillment of a childhood pledge. He had vowed to do something monumental for the Church when he grew up if his mother was spared possible death following a difficult birth of a little girl. Years passed, and the lad became a Servite priest. He never forgot his promise, and when the opportunity presented itself in 1923 in the form of a large piece of property held by the Union Pacific Railroad in northeast Portland, he saw the potential and arranged for the purchase of the property. He immedi-

The Grotto, a peaceful sixty-two-acre retreat near the center of Portland, features a marble replica of Michelangelo's famous *Pietà*. (*The Grotto—National Sanctuary of Our Sorrowful Mother*)

ately began clearing the two levels of property separated by a hundred-foot cliff, and the shrine opened in 1924, dedicated to Our Sorrowful Mother.

PRAYER OF INTERCESSION TO OUR SORROWFUL MOTHER

Let intercession be made for us, we beseech you, O Lord Jesus Christ, now and at the hour of our death, before the throne of your mercy, by the Blessed Virgin Mary, your Mother, whose most holy soul was pierced by a sword of sorrow in the hour of your bitter passion. Through you, Jesus Christ, Savior of the world, who with the Father and the Holy Spirit live and reign world without end. Amen.

ABOUT THE SHRINE

No visit to Portland would be complete without a trip to The Grotto. It is an internationally renowned Catholic sanctuary that welcomes more than 150,000 guests of all faiths each year. Pilgrims to The Grotto are delighted to discover the peaceful sixty-two-acre retreat near the center of the city. Lush green forests tower over colorful rhododendron and other native Pacific Northwest flora along the walks toward the central plaza and the heart of the sanctuary—Our Lady's Grotto: a magnificent rock cave carved into the base of a 110-foot cliff. A marble replica of Michelangelo's famous *Pietà* is featured in its center. On the upper level, the manicured gardens offer magnificent panoramic vistas of the Columbia River Valley, the Cascade Range, and famous Mount St. Helens. Especially impressive is the 180-foot floor-to-ceiling view through the beveled glass wall of the spectacular Meditation Chapel. Other highlights include the Servite Monastery, a life-size bronze statue of Saint Francis of Assisi, the streams and reflection ponds of the Peace Garden, and the *Via Matris,* which offers superb examples of wood sculpture.

SHRINE INFORMATION

The Grotto
The Order of the Servants of Mary
P.O. Box 20008
Portland, OR 97294-0008
(503) 254-7371
fax: (503) 254-7948

TOURIST INFORMATION

Hotels and motels are plentiful in the immediate area, including Quality Inn (82nd and Sandy Boulevard), Airport Sheraton, Airport Holiday Inn, and Days Inn-Airport. Many others are within five to ten minutes of the shrine. At The Grotto, pilgrims can enjoy specialty beverages and lunches or snacks inside the Welcome Center or in the outdoor garden setting.

Directions to the Shrine

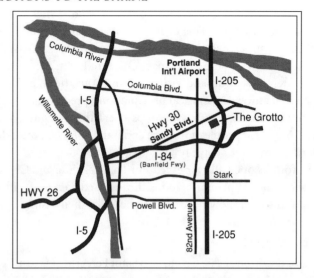

The Grotto is conveniently located on Sandy Boulevard (Highway 30) at NE 85th Avenue, a half mile west of I-205, just minutes from downtown and from Portland International Airport. Ample free parking for cars and tour buses is available.

FROM THE AIRPORT

Take Airport Way to 82nd Avenue, turning left to Sandy Boulevard, and left to 85th Avenue.

FROM DOWNTOWN PORTLAND

Take I-84 east to 82nd Avenue and follow the airport sign to Sandy Boulevard. Turn right to 85th Avenue.

For First-Time Pilgrims

A seasonal feature of The Grotto is a Sunday outdoor Mass celebrated from the first Sunday in May to the end of September. Other devotional services are celebrated, such as an outdoor evening Mass and rosary procession on the Feast of the Assumption. A Mother's Day Mass in May draws large crowds to honor mothers living and deceased. On the Sunday closest to our American Independence Day, the Vietnamese Community of Portland sponsors a Freedom Day Mass celebrating freedom from the oppression of bygone years and invites other cultures to join on that day. This is the largest annual celebration at the shrine each summer, drawing thousands from the West Coast states. The winter season sees the Christmas Festival of Lights, which attracts approximately fifty thousand visitors throughout the month of December and features 125 musical presentations, predominately choirs from schools, churches, and civic groups, over a thirty-night span. This is a local "must" for people of the area and is the only religious celebration of Christmas for people of all faiths.

The Grotto is open all year except on Thanksgiving and Christmas Day. Visitors should plan on walking through sixty acres of pathways, gardens, and so on, allowing at least an hour for their visit.

OF SPECIAL INTEREST

A major devotion at The Grotto is to Saint Peregrine Laziosi, O.S.M., universal patron of those who suffer from cancer, AIDS, Alzheimer's Disease, and related life-threatening diseases. A monthly Mass is celebrated, with veneration of the relic of the saint by all present.

Shrine of Our Lady of Fátima
LATON, CALIFORNIA

Fátima, Portugal, was a quiet little place in the early years of this century, a place where the local inhabitants earned their living primarily by shepherding and farming. In addition, it was a place where the Catholic faith was strong and where the rosary was prayed often. It was here, on May 13, 1917, that the first of seven apparitions of our Blessed Mother occurred to three peasant children: Lúcia, Francisco, and Jacinta. Their "beautiful lady" is now known to us as Our Lady of Fátima.

Fátima is well known as the place where our Blessed Lady delivered "three secrets" to the children. The first secret: "I promise salvation to those who embrace devotion to my Immaculate Heart. Their souls will be loved by God as flowers placed by me to adorn his throne. These souls will suffer a great deal but I will never leave them. My Immaculate Heart will be their refuge, the way that will lead them to God."

The second secret of Fátima: "You have seen hell where poor sinners go. To save them, God wishes to establish in the world devotion to my Immaculate Heart. If what I say to you is done, many souls will be saved and there will be peace in the world." This second secret also contained a request that Russia be consecrated to the Immaculate Heart of Mary and that a Communion of reparation be received by all the faithful on the first Saturday of each month.

The third secret of Fátima has never been revealed, although some people believe that the apparitions that occurred in Akita, Japan, on October 13, 1973, essentially revealed this third secret. This apparition reportedly contained a divine warning for the entire world.

ROSARY PRAYER OF OUR LADY OF FÁTIMA

O my Jesus, forgive us our sins, save us from the fires of hell, and lead all souls to heaven, especially those in need of thy mercy. Amen.

ABOUT THE SHRINE

The Shrine of Our Lady of Fátima was constructed in 1953, just thirty-six years after the first apparition at Fátima. The construction of the shrine and the church vividly illustrates the hold that the Fátima experience had on Catholic people of the time. Today, some forty-five years later, it still serves as the only shrine to Our Lady in the diocese of Fresno, California. The shrine has also served as a parish church since the same date.

SHRINE INFORMATION

The Shrine of Our Lady of Fátima
20855 Fátima Avenue
P.O. Box 119
Laton, CA 93242
(209) 923-4935
fax: (209) 923-CATH

TOURIST INFORMATION

Specific information regarding overnight lodging and meals can be obtained by writing to the above address.

DIRECTIONS TO THE SHRINE

The Shrine of Our Lady of Fátima is located about twenty miles south of Fresno in the agricultural heart of California. State Hwy. 41, exiting east on East Mount Whitney into Laton, may be the best route.

FOR FIRST-TIME PILGRIMS

A priest is available to celebrate Mass and hear confessions in English, Portuguese, and Spanish. Religious groups are invited to use the shrine for day retreats and special times of prayer. Because of changing schedules and the daily routine of parish life, it is best to call ahead for Mass times and for a current calendar of activities.

OF SPECIAL INTEREST

Special celebrations for Our Blessed Mother include a Portuguese Feast of Our Lady of Fátima in May on Mother's Day, a multicultural celebration of Our Lady of Fátima in October, and a Spanish celebration of Our Lady of Guadalupe on December 12 each year. From May through October pilgrims may participate in a special Mass and procession with Our Blessed Mother on the thirteenth of each month to commemorate the apparitions of Our Lady in 1917 at Fátima, Portugal. Other special celebrations are held at the shrine for Epiphany, during Holy Week, and on the Feast of Saint Anthony.

Midwest Region

Basilica and National Shrine of Our Lady of Consolation

CONVENTUAL FRANCISCAN FRIARS
CAREY, OHIO

Since 1875 countless thousands of pilgrims have journeyed to this shrine to express their devotion to Mary, Consoler of the Afflicted. Saint Ignatius of Antioch first expressed devotion to Mary as Consoler of the Afflicted in the second century when he wrote, "Mary, knowing what it is to suffer, is ever ready to administer consolation."

In the seventeenth century when an outbreak of bubonic plague in the Grand Duchy of Luxembourg ravaged and decimated its population, the people formed a spiritual union to pray to Mary, Consoler of the Afflicted for relief in their anguish and fear of death. Under the spiritual leadership of Father Brodquart, a Jesuit teacher of Luxembourg, a small chapel was built on the outskirts of the town and an image of Mary, Consoler of the Afflicted was enshrined there. Many favors and several authenticated miracles occurred among the visiting pilgrims. And on January 27, 1652, Pope Innocent X, in order to foster devotion to the Blessed Virgin under the title of Our Lady of Consolation, es-

The statue of Our Lady of Consolation is taken from the upper basilica every Sunday from May through October for an outdoor rosary procession. *(Basilica and National Shrine of Our Lady of Consolation)*

tablished a confraternity at the little shrine. The great increase in the number of pilgrims coming from many lands made it necessary to take the image and the devotion to the cathedral in the city of Luxembourg.

Here Our Lady of Consolation became the patroness of the Duchy of Luxembourg.

The devotion flourished for two hundred years, then spread to North America, where Fr. Joseph P. Gloden established the first shrine at the mission of Carey, Ohio, which was attached to his Church of St. Nicholas at nearby Frenchtown. The people of Carey, influenced by the fervor and enthusiasm of Father Gloden, a native of Luxembourg, agreed to complete a new frame church and dedicate it to Mary, Consoler of the Afflicted. Accordingly, a replica of the original image at Luxembourg Cathedral was brought to Frenchtown; and from there a solemn procession took it to the little church at Carey. On April 28, 1878, Pope Leo XIII established a confraternity at Carey, similar to that at the mother church in Luxembourg, thus firmly establishing the devotion of Our Lady of Consolation in this country.

PRAYER TO OUR LADY OF CONSOLATION

Holy Mary, Mother of Jesus, Consoler of the Afflicted, I place myself this day under your special protection, and I invoke your motherly aid. I promise to be faithful to your Divine Son, and to honor you with my whole heart. Accept me, I implore you, as your child, and protect me now and forever. Ever guide my footsteps; comfort me in my pain and grief; teach me through life to do the will of God; and be with me in the hour of my death. Amen.

ABOUT THE SHRINE

The little church, beloved by all who come to Carey, still stands and is used for special devotions. Today, the image of Our Lady of Consolation is enshrined in a superstructure consisting of an upper church, which houses the statue, and a lower church, which holds the evidence of the cures of the many sick, crippled, and maimed who have begged and received aid and grace from Our Lady of Consolation. These braces, canes, crutches, and even beer cans are displayed there, as well as many of the dresses in Our Lady's wardrobe (all donated by devotees), including a vestment sent by Pope Paul VI.

Shrine Park, thirty acres of beautifully landscaped lawn, trees, and shrubs, is home to an imposing marble and granite altar—a memorial to the sons and daughters who gave their lives in the Second World War and to all the deceased who are beloved by the friends of the shrine. Atop the golden dome of this magnificent structure stands a giant replica of the image of Our Lady of Consolation—visible for miles—a beacon for all to come and pray. The stone grottoes marking the Way of the Cross and several exquisite religious statues, all gifts of grateful pilgrims and friends of the shrine, add much to the feeling of reverence you will experience as you stroll through this beautiful park.

SHRINE INFORMATION

Basilica and National Shrine of Our Lady of Consolation
315 Clay Street
Carey, OH 43316
(419) 396-7107
fax: (419) 396-3355

TOURIST INFORMATION

Specific information regarding restaurants and lodging can be obtained by contacting the shrine office at the above address. The Saint Anthony Pilgrim House offers accommodations for overnight pilgrims. The Sisters of Saint Francis are the administrators, and reservations should be made in writing to them. The shrine cafeteria is also available for special groups.

DIRECTIONS TO THE SHRINE

The shrine is located in Carey, Ohio, south of Toledo, and is easily accessible from most major highways.

FOR FIRST-TIME PILGRIMS

The Shrine of Our Lady of Consolation and Shrine Park are handicapped accessible. Smooth, winding roadways leading though Shrine Park mark the Way of the Cross. Those with infirmities can easily make their way by car, bus, or wheelchair. During the summer, members of the Franciscan Friars (in charge of the shrine) lead pilgrims in the devotions of the Stations of the Cross. Every Sunday afternoon during the summer, pilgrims are invited to walk in solemn procession behind the miraculous image of Our Lady to Shrine Park for special services.

Each service includes the Benediction of the Most Blessed Sacrament, blessing with the relic of the true cross, and the blessing of the sick. August is the most popular month for pilgrimages, a special novena being preached August 6 through 15 in preparation for the Feast of the Assumption of the Blessed Virgin. The Renewal Center is available for retreats year-round. There are special retreats for husbands and wives, teenagers, and other groups when the schedule allows. Write to the retreat director for specific information.

OF SPECIAL INTEREST

The miraculous image of Our Lady of Consolation was brought to Carey from the mother shrine at Luxembourg in 1875. Relics of wood and cloth from the original image hang around the neck of the Carey image. The jewels and precious metals in the crowns were donated by grateful pilgrims and devotees.

The Black Madonna Shrine and Grottoes
FRANCISCAN MISSIONARY BROTHERS
EUREKA, MISSOURI

My grace shall accompany it.

The picture of Our Lady of Czestochowa at the Black Madonna Shrine and Grottoes near Eureka, Missouri, is a true copy of the world-famous miraculous picture located at the Jasna Gora Monastery in Poland. The copy was commissioned in 1960 by Stefan Cardinal Wyszynski, blessed, touched to the original picture, and erected in her honor by Brother Bronislaus Luszcz, O.S.F., of the Franciscan Missionary Brothers.

It is doubtful whether any other representation of Our Blessed Mother with her Divine Child possesses a more ancient and glorious history than the picture of Our Lady of Czestochowa. Tradition tells us that Saint Luke painted it on the top of the cypress wood table that was built by Saint Joseph and used by the Holy Family at Nazareth, and that Mary sat for the painting at the request of the early Christians. It was renowned for its miracles and venerated for three hundred years while hidden in Jerusalem.

Saint Helena brought it to Constantinople, where it was honored for five hundred years, then given as a wedding gift by the Byzantine emperor to a Greek princess and a Ruthenian nobleman. They carried it to the city of Kiev in what is now the Ukraine, where it remained in the Royal Palace of Belz for 579 years.

In 1382 the picture received its first injury from invading Tartars. An arrow pieced it, leaving a scar on the neck that is still visible. So Prince Ladislaus Opolski decided to move the miraculous image to one of his castles in Upper Silesia. However, within a few paces of the small village of Czestochowa, on the brow of a hill called Jasna Gora, the horses drawing the wagon carrying the picture stopped, and no amount of coaxing or goading could make them go on. The prince took the horses' balking as a sign from Our Lady that this spot was to be her new home. There he built a massive fortress-monastery and in its chapel solemnly enthroned Our Lady of Czestochowa, entrusting it to the care

The grottoes at the Black Madonna Shrine and Grottoes are constructed of Missouri tiff rock but include rocks, sea shells, and costume jewelry that were donated by pilgrims or sent from the foreign missions. *(Anthony F. Chiffolo)*

of the Basilian monks of the Greek Rite. A few years later, however, Prince Opolski gave it over to the Latin Rite Hermits of St. Paul, who are still in Czestochowa.

The year 1382 begins the remarkable recorded history of this miraculous picture. It figured in the heroic, successful defense of Poland against invaders who were enemies of the Church: the Swedes in 1655, the Turks in 1683, and the Bolsheviks in 1920. As a result, Our Lady of Czestochowa was officially proclaimed Queen of Poland.

During all these stirring historical events the picture did not escape desecration and mutilation. In 1430, during the Hussites' unsuccessful attempt to carry it off, the picture was broken and the face slashed with sabers. Repeated efforts to patch the scars by skilled artists failed. The facial cuts reappeared, and they are clearly shown on the right cheek of the Blessed Mother. In 1909 vandals tore off the gold crown and "overdress" of pearls. This sacrilege was repaired with the help of the pope, Saint Pius X, who furnished a new crown.

Pope after pope has granted spiritual favors to pilgrims to the shrine and enriched it with many privileges. At present a picture of Our Lady of Czestochowa adorns the altar of the pope's private chapel at Castol Gondolfo.

ABOUT THE SHRINE

The Black Madonna Shrine and Grottoes are a shining example of what one man with faith can achieve. Located in the beautiful foothills of the Ozarks, this peaceful, refreshing place is a welcome tonic for the body as well as the soul. The grottoes are constructed of Missouri tiff rock, and everything that can be seen—rocks, sea shells, and costume jewelry—was donated by visitors or sent from the foreign missions. The unique outdoor Chapel of the Hills, with its beautiful mosaics created by world-renowned artist Frederick Hence, is home to paintings of the Miraculous Image of Our Lady of Czestochowa. The grottoes are dedicated to the Stations of the Cross, the Seven Joys of Mary, Saint Francis, Saint Joseph, Our Lady of Perpetual Help, Our Lady of Sorrows, the Assumption, the Nativity, and the Garden of Gethsemane.

SHRINE INFORMATION

The Black Madonna of Czestochowa Shrine and Grottoes
St. Joseph Road
Eureka, MO 63025
(314) 938-5361

TOURIST INFORMATION

Overnight lodging can be arranged by contacting the above address. Bus groups and pilgrimages are welcome. The shrine offers catered meals to groups of thirty or more pilgrims with prior arrangement.

DIRECTIONS TO THE SHRINE

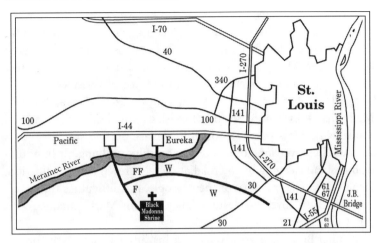

The Black Madonna Shrine and Grottoes are located in the greater St. Louis area, in the foothills of the Ozarks.

From downtown St. Louis, take I-44 west to the Eureka exit, turn south onto Hwy. 2, and drive to Hwy. FF. Turn right onto Hwy. FF and drive to Hwy. F. Make a left turn onto Hwy. F, drive to St. Joseph's Road, continue until you come to the shrine entrance, and turn left. (From I-44 to the shrine is approximately eight miles.)

FOR FIRST-TIME PILGRIMS

The shrine is open from April through September at 9:00 A.M. until 7:00 P.M.; during October and March from 9:00 A.M. until 5:00 P.M.; and from November through February from 9:00 A.M. until 4:00 P.M. Mass is celebrated weekly at 10:00 A.M. in the Sacred Heart Chapel of Our Lady of the Angels Monastery. The entrance to the chapel is accessible from the rear parking lot of St. Joseph Hill Infirmary. There are no services on weekdays. Pilgrims are also invited to visit the shrine gift shop, which offers a wide selection of religious gifts and information on the Black Madonna Shrine and Our Lady of Czestochowa. The gift shop is open daily, except for Christmas Day and Thanksgiving.

OF SPECIAL INTEREST

Brother Bronislaus, a Franciscan Brother who emigrated from Poland, was a man driven by an overwhelming faith and love for Our Blessed Mother Mary. In his native Poland, Mary is revered as the Queen of Peace and Mercy, and her most famous shrine is at a monastery called Jasna Gora ("Bright Hill") in the town of Czestochowa. The people lovingly refer to Mary as Our Lady of Czestochowa, the Black Madonna. In his youth, Brother Bronislaus would sit by the road and watch as pilgrims passed through his village on their way to Mary's shrine. They overcame tremendous hardships, walking for hundreds of miles and sleeping by the road at night to reach their destination, Jasna Gora. The memory of these people, the difficulties they overcame, and the love and devotion they had for Mary remained with him throughout his life.

Brother Bronislaus wanted to share his faith with others by spreading the glory of Our Lady of Czestochowa. So in 1937 he began his lifetime labor of love. Clearing the thickly wooded land, he built a beautiful cedarwood chapel and hung a picture of Our Lady about the altar. The chapel soon became a center of religious devotion, with numerous pilgrimages, prayer services, and Masses being offered. The Chapel of the Hills, dedicated to Our Lady of Czestochowa, was erected in the 1960s to replace the original cedarwood chapel that was burned to the ground by arsonists. Brother Bronislaus continued with his life's labor by erecting seven grottoes, each incorporating his ingenuity and craftsmanship in their intricate designs. Some are constructed with jewelry trinkets and homeland souvenirs left by visitors from all the states and other countries who came to see the shrine.

Fátima Family Apostolate

IMMACULATE HEART MESSENGER
ALEXANDRIA, SOUTH DAKOTA

The shrine honoring the Holy Family and the holy Eucharist was the fulfillment of the dream of Fr. Robert J. Fox, known in the United States and beyond as the "Fátima Priest." This priest founded the Fátima Family Apostolate, which is recognized by the Pontifical Council for the Family. In 1987 Father Fox built the outdoor shrine, where Mass can be offered and candlelight processions held. Father Fox still directs the shrine.

PRAYER TO THE IMMACULATE VIRGIN

Immaculate Virgin, who being conceived without sin directed every movement of your most pure heart toward God, and was always submissive to his divine will, obtain for me the grace to hate sin with all my heart and to learn from you to live in perfect resignation to the will of God. Amen.

ABOUT THE SHRINE

The shrine was built from the royalties of the many books and articles written by Father Fox over a period of thirty-some years. The shrine is home to the international Fátima Family Apostolate, dedicated to the sanctification of the family. Located on the extensive rural shrine

The shrine honoring the Holy Family and the holy Eucharist is located on the grounds of the Fátima Family Apostolate, which is dedicated to the sanctification of the family. *(Fátima Family Apostolate)*

grounds is St. Mary of Mercy Church, containing sites honoring the King of Divine Mercy, Our Lady of Guadalupe, and Our Lady of Fátima.

The second weekend of each June, Friday through Sunday, a National Marian Congress at the shrine draws thousands with its focus on the call of the family to holiness.

SHRINE INFORMATION

> Fátima Family Apostolate
> P.O. Box 158
> Alexandria, SD 57311-0158
> (605) 239-4532

TOURIST INFORMATION

Hotel accommodations are available just fifteen minutes away in Mitchell.

DIRECTIONS TO THE SHRINE

Fátima Family Apostolate, located in the world's only corn palace, is twelve miles east of Mitchell and fifty-five miles west of Sioux Falls on I-90.

FOR FIRST–TIME PILGRIMS

Visitors to the outdoor shrine can make the Stations of the Cross, consecrate their families at the outdoor Holy Family Chapel, and pray before the Pro-Life Shrine of Our Lady of Guadalupe and before an image of the Angel of the Family, both with special inscribed prayers at their bases.

The beautiful shrine attracted the building of the first contemplative Carmelite monastery in South Dakota in 1997. Mother of Mercy Carmel is located next to the shrine area, and Mass is offered daily in its beautiful chapel, with the nuns singing Gregorian chant on Sundays. The Carmelite Sisters offer a store featuring the many books, audiotapes, and video albums of the Fátima Family Apostolate.

Daily Mass is at 7:30 A.M. in the Carmel Chapel. Sunday Mass is at 7:30 A.M. in the Carmel Chapel and 9:30 A.M. in the Shrine Church, which holds three hundred people and is an extension to the outdoor shrine.

Confessions are heard Saturdays at 7:30 and 8:30 P.M. and Sundays at 9:30 A.M.

OF SPECIAL INTEREST

The Shrine has drawn the bishops of Leiria-Fátima in Portugal on three occasions, the cardinal prefect of the Pontifical Council of the Family, the Catholic archbishop from Moscow, Russia, and thousands of visitors each year. From here were raised the funds for the construction in 1997 of the first Shrine to Our Lady of Fátima in Russia located in St. Petersburg.

The Grotto

DICKEYVILLE, WISCONSIN

The Grotto and shrines erected in the village of Dickeyville, Wisconsin, on Holy Ghost Parish grounds are the works of Fr. Matthias Wernerus, a Catholic priest, pastor of the parish from 1918 to 1931. His handiwork in stone, built from 1925 to 1930, is dedicated to the unity of two great American ideals—love of God and love of country. It is a creation in stone, mortar, and bright colored objects—collected materials from all over the world. These include colored glass, gems, antique heirlooms of pottery or porcelain, stalagmites and stalac-

The Grotto is a creation in stone, mortar, and bright colored objects—collected materials from all over the world. *(The Grotto)*

tites, sea shells of all kinds, starfish, petrified sea urchins and fossils, and a variety of corals plus amber glass, agate, quartz, ores such as iron, copper, lead, fool's gold, rock crystals, onyx, amethyst, and coal. Many items are antiques. You will even find petrified wood and moss. And there are many of those round balls that used to be found on the top of a stick shift in old cars. This religious and patriotic shrine was constructed without the use of blueprints.

TRADITIONAL CLOSING PRAYER OF THE ANGELUS

Pour forth, we beseech thee, O Lord, thy grace into our hearts; that we, as we have known the Incarnation of Christ thy Son by the message of an angel, so by his passion and cross we may be brought to the glory of his Resurrection, through the same Christ, our Lord. Amen.

ABOUT THE SHRINE

SHRINE INFORMATION

The Dickeyville Grotto
305 West Main Street
P.O. Box 429
Dickeyville, WI 53808-0429
(608) 568-3119

TOURIST INFORMATION

The village of Dickeyville has a population of one thousand. It has two motels, several restaurants, parks, two schools, and many small businesses. Pilgrims may dine at Mueller's Restaurant, Valentine's Restaurant, or Sunset Lanes and Hall. Overnight lodging can be obtained at Plaza Motel (Highways 35-61 & 151) or Tower Motel (Highways 35-61 & 151). There are also picnic tables at The Grotto (near the gift shop) for pilgrims' use.

DIRECTIONS TO THE SHRINE

The Grotto is located in Dickeyville in southwestern Wisconsin about twelve miles north of Dubuque, Iowa. It is easily reached by traveling north from Dubuque on State Hwy. 151.

FOR FIRST-TIME PILGRIMS

There are several shrines in The Grotto garden. Besides the main shrine, which houses the Grotto of the Blessed Virgin, there is a patriotic shrine, the Sacramental Shrine of the Holy Eucharist, the Sacred Heart Shrine, Christ the King Shrine, and the Stations of the Cross. These shrines are located in a beautiful floral garden area surrounding the Holy Ghost Church.

The Grotto offers guided tours from June 1 through August 31, seven days a week from 9:00 A.M. to 5:00 P.M. Tours are available on weekends only in May, September, and October.

OF SPECIAL INTEREST

The Los Angeles organization known as SPACES (Saving and Preserving Arts and Cultural Environment) has classified this work, the Dickeyville Grotto, as "environmental folk art." Individuals interested in this type of art have made inquiries from all parts of the United States.

Grotto of the Redemption
WEST BEND, IOWA

The Grotto of Bethlehem at the Grotto of the Redemption, which is the largest grotto in the world. *(Grotto of the Redemption)*

The story of how the Grotto came into being is as moving as are the scenes it portrays. It is generally told as a fact that as a young seminarian Fr. Paul Matthias Dobberstein, who emigrated to America from Germany in 1892, became critically ill with pneumonia. As he fought for his life, he prayed to the Blessed Virgin to intercede for him. He promised to build a shrine in her honor if he lived. The illness passed, the student completed his studies, and after his ordination he came to West Bend, Iowa, as pastor in 1898. For more than a decade he stockpiled rocks and precious stones. The actual work of giving permanence to his promise began to take shape in 1912. The designed purpose of the Grotto is to tell, in silent stone made spiritually eloquent, the story of humankind's fall and redemption by Christ, the Savior of the World.

PRAYER TO THE HOLY MOTHER OF GOD

We fly to your patronage, O holy Mother of God; despise not our petitions in our necessities, but deliver us always from all dangers, O glorious and Blessed Virgin. Amen.

ABOUT THE SHRINE

The love of precious stones is deeply implanted in the human heart, and the cause of this must be sought not only in their coloring and brilliancy but also in their durability. All the fair colors of flowers and foliage, even the blue of the sky and the glory of sunset clouds, last for only a short time and are subject to continual change, but the sheen and color of precious stones are the same today as they were thousands of years ago and will be for countless years to come. In a world of change, this permanence has a charm of its own that was appreciated early in the history of humankind and remains to this day.

It is evident from his work that Father Dobberstein was a great lover of beauty. In fulfilling his vows to erect a shrine to the Mother of Christ he was determined to make the most of material beauty and to emphasize the spiritual beauty of the woman he had in mind. It was his purpose that others might see in the beauty of stone the beauty of the Creator and by being charmed and attracted by his work learn to imitate the virtues of the Mother of our Savior.

The Grotto of the Redemption is the largest grotto in the world. It is frequently considered "the Eighth Wonder of the World." It represents the largest collection of minerals and petrification concentrated in any one spot in the world. The Grotto has an estimated geological value of more than $2.5 million.

Father Dobberstein started construction on the Grotto in 1912, and for forty-two years, winter and summer, he labored to set ornamental rocks and gems into concrete. When in 1954 he died, the incredible "Grotto of the Redemption" he had created covered one city block. It is a composite of nine separate grottoes—each portraying some scene in the life of Christ and his work of redeeming the world.

SHRINE INFORMATION

Grotto of the Redemption
300 N. Broadway
Box 376
West Bend, IA 50597
(515) 887-2371 (phone)
(515) 887-2372 (fax)
Internet home page: www.okoboji.com/Attractions/Grotto
e-mail: grotto@ncn.net

TOURIST INFORMATION

A restaurant on the grounds of the Grotto (open May 1–October 15) is famous for its home-cooked meals. Large groups can make reservations by calling (515) 887-2371. There is free overnight camping with eighty electrical hookups available from April through October. Facilities on the grounds include modern rest rooms with showers and an RV dumping station. Accommodations may also be found at the West Bend Motel by calling (515) 887-3611. Private vehicles, public transit, motor coaches, and mobile homes all have easy access and nearby parking.

DIRECTIONS TO THE SHRINE

West Bend is located in the center of a vast, lush, level expanse of Iowan farmland about one hundred miles northwest of Des Moines and about thirty-five miles northwest of Ft. Dodge, not far from busy State Hwy. 18 to the north. The surrounding area is populated by wise, industrious, and fairly prosperous farmers.

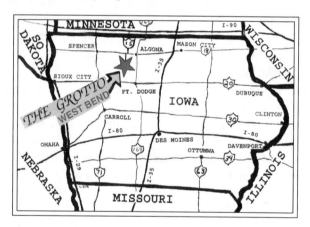

FROM DES MOINES

Take I-35 north to the Clear Lake area, then go west on Rte. 18, then south on Rte. 15 for about eight miles. The entrance to the shrine is on the right.

FROM FT. DODGE

Head north on Hwy. 169, then go west on B63 for ten miles.

FROM SIOUX CITY

Head north on Rte. 75 to Le Mars, then go east on Rte. 3. At Humboldt, go north on Rte. 169, then go west on B63 for ten miles.

FROM MINNEAPOLIS

Travel south on I-35, then take I-90 west to the Fairmont area. Head south on Hwy. 15. The entrance to the shrine is about eight miles past the Rte. 18 intersection.

FOR FIRST–TIME PILGRIMS

Videocassettes, slides, and books that offer explanations and pictorial guides of the grotto are available by writing to the address above or by visiting the gift shop and museum. Mass is celebrated each Saturday at 5:00 P.M. and on Sundays during the summer at 9:00 A.M. (during the winter at 9:30 A.M.). Group Masses and prayer services are arranged upon request. In addition, guided tours are available daily from May 15–October 15. The suggested donation is $3.00 per adult.

OF SPECIAL INTEREST

Most architects and contractors would hesitate a long time before undertaking a project such as the Grotto of the Redemption at West Bend, Iowa. It is doubtful whether it can or ever will be duplicated. The sheer bulk of the achievement is startling when we consider that two men did most of the manual labor and Father Dobberstein accomplished practically all of the artistic endeavor single-handedly.

There are almost a hundred carloads of rocks and stones, the vast bulk of which had to be minutely processed, stored, classified, and handled many times before it found its final and proper place in the harmonious structure. No accounting was made either of the many hours of labor involved in building the grotto or of the money expended in gathering stones and shaping them into a harmonious unit. This is perhaps because Father Dobberstein wanted the cost to be known to God alone. One of the most amazing things about the grotto at West Bend is the great tenacity of purpose the builder displayed in carrying out his plans. Indeed, it is the largest known accomplishment of its kind anywhere in the world!

$$+\!\!\!\parallel\!\!+$$
$$+\!\!\!\parallel\!\!+$$

Immaculate Heart of Mary Shrine
CONGREGATION OF THE MOTHER CO-REDEMPTRIX
CARTHAGE, MISSOURI

The Immaculate Heart of Mary Shrine was formerly known as "Our Lady of Fátima," and the property was previously owned by the Oblates of Mary Immaculate. Built in 1959, in honor of Our Lady of Fátima, the shrine became a retreat center for Catholics from the neighboring states. About 1971, due to the rising crisis of religious vocations throughout the Church, and in particular within the Oblate religious community, all the activities of the shrine were entrusted to the board of directors of Our Lady of the Snows in Belleville, Illinois. After that time, the shrine became unfrequented and less active.

In June 1975, through the mysterious workings of God's loving providence, the religious of the Congregation of the Mother

Co-Redemptrix, sponsored by the Most Rev. Bernard F. Law, then bishop of Springfield-Cape Girardeau, settled at this institution. Now the shrine is open every day for these refugee religious to praise and honor their heavenly Mother.

In May 1981, the Oblates ceded ownership of the shrine to the Congregation of the

The Immaculate Heart of Mary Shrine is well known to almost all the Vietnamese in the United States and throughout the world, and to many other ethnic groups as well.
(Immaculate Heart of Mary Shrine)

Mother Co-Redemptrix religious community, which is now established as a province of the Congregation of the Mother Co-Redemptrix in the United States. The shrine was given the new title "The Immaculate Heart of Mary Shrine" in response to the Oblates' wish that the shrine be renamed. The Congregation of the Mother Co-Redemptrix Fathers and Brothers chose this name because this religious family, from its beginning, has worked to spread devotion to the Immaculate Heart of Mary wherever its members are present. The Immaculate Heart of Mary Shrine is now well known to almost all the Vietnamese in the United States and throughout the world, and to many other ethnic groups in this country.

PRAYER TO THE HEART OF MARY

O heart of Mary, Mother of God and our Mother; heart most worthy of our love, in which the adorable Trinity is ever well-pleased, worthy of the veneration and love of all the angels and of all humanity; heart most like the heart of Jesus, of which you are the perfect image; heart, full of goodness, ever compassionate toward our miseries; deign to melt our icy hearts and grant that they may be changed into the likeness of your Son. Amen.

ABOUT THE SHRINE

The Shrine of the Immaculate Heart of Mary is a shrine with great purpose. Among other activities, the shrine serves the Church community in the following ways:

- To preserve and strengthen devotion to the Immaculate Heart of Mary, encouraging the faithful to respond positively to the three requests of Our Lady of Fátima. Besides a monthly newsletter, with editions each month in English and in Vietnamese, the shrine also publishes and reprints Catholic literature to help deepen faith in God and in the Blessed Virgin Mary.
- To pray for the needs of all who seek help from God and Our Blessed Mother through the Congregation of the Mother Co-Redemptrix apostolate.

- To serve as a retreat center for any who need spiritual refreshment.
- To serve as a Marian pilgrim center, where the community holds the annual Marian Day Celebration for people from throughout the United States and the world. (On the first Marian Day Celebration in 1978, fifteen hundred Vietnamese Catholics from nearby communities gathered to express together their filial devotion to the Blessed Mother and to pray for religious freedom in their native country, Vietnam. The number of participants increases every year, and since 1986 annual attendance has exceeded forty thousand!)
- To sponsor the annual Christmas light show called "The Way of Salvation." Every year thousands of people visit the shrine to travel through corridors of glowing lights depicting the paradise of Adam and Eve, the great flood and Noah's Ark, the willing sacrifice of Abraham, a caravan of travelers journeying to Bethlehem City, and finally the scene of the newborn baby Jesus with Mary and Joseph. For the Congregation of the Mother Co-Redemptrix community, "The Way of Salvation" is a way to remind people of the total story of this world's salvation, and the context in which the miracle of the Nativity took place.

SHRINE INFORMATION

Immaculate Heart of Mary Shrine
1900 Grand Avenue
Carthage, MO 64836-3500
(417) 358-8580

TOURIST INFORMATION

Although small and simple, the Immaculate Heart of Mary Shrine has some comfortable facilities for guests who wish to stay overnight. There are double bedrooms for about fifteen persons, and fairly large parking lots.

DIRECTIONS TO THE SHRINE

The Immaculate Heart of Mary Shrine is in southwest Missouri, about ten miles northeast of Joplin and fifty-four miles west of Springfield.

FROM SPRINGFIELD

Take I-44 west to exit 57, then take Rte. 96 west to Carthage.

FROM JOPLIN

Take I-44 east to exit 18, then take Rte. 71 north to Carthage.

FOR FIRST-TIME PILGRIMS

Besides the annual Marian Day Celebration, which is usually held in August, and the novenas according to the seasonal events in every month, the shrine has no specific schedules of its own. The guests of the shrine usually follow the schedules of the Congregation of the Mother Co-Redemptrix religious community, which includes morning prayer and Eucharist, daytime and evening prayer, and Holy Hour and Eucharistic Benediction. Sundays and holidays as well as special occasions have their own schedules.

OF SPECIAL INTEREST

The Congregation of the Mother Co-Redemptrix (C.M.C.) is a clerical institute of consecrated life begun in 1941 in North Vietnam. In 1954, with the Treaty of Geneva that divided Vietnam into two parts (North and South) and placed North Vietnam under the rule of the Vietnam communist government, the congregation had to move to South Vietnam to escape religious persecution. In the South, under God's providential love and the Blessed Virgin Mary's motherly care and protection, the congregation spread rapidly in various dioceses. The missionary work of the congregation was not only fertile at its mission centers in those dioceses, it was also fruitful in the other institutions established and conducted by its members. These included elementary and high schools, residences for college students, homes for retired priests, shelters for the poor and homeless, and so on.

When the Vietnamese communists took over South Vietnam in 1975, a large number of C.M.C. members came to the United States. Under the sponsorship of His Eminence Bernard Cardinal Law, then bishop of Springfield-Cape Girardeau, they resettled in Carthage, Missouri. On October 25, 1980, the Holy See erected the first province of the institute outside Vietnam, the United States Assumption Province for all religious members in America. This province has more than 170 members working in more than twenty archdioceses and dioceses in this country. The priests serve as pastors, associate pastors in both American and Vietnamese parishes, and chaplains in hospitals and to the Vietnamese communities.

$$+\!\!\!\parallel\!\!\!+$$

Mary Immaculate Queen National Shrine
ST. PIUS X CATHOLIC CHURCH
LOMBARD, ILLINOIS

On October 11, 1954, Pope Pius XII established the Feast of the Queenship of Mary to be celebrated throughout the world, and commanded that on that date each year the world should renew its consecration to her. The feast is celebrated on August 22. "The purpose of the feast is that all may recognize more clearly and venerate more devoutly the merciful and motherly sovereignty of her who bore God in her womb" (Pius XII, *Ad. Coeli Reginam*).

On the day of her Assumption, Mary our Mother was solemnly crowned by Christ and received by the whole court of heaven as Queen.

PRAYER TO MARY, QUEEN OF HEAVEN

O Mary Immaculate Queen, look down upon this distressed and suffering world. You know our misery and our weakness. O you who are our Mother, saving us in the hour of peril, have compassion on us in these days of great and heavy trial. Jesus has confided to you the treasure of his grace, and through you he wills to grant us pardon and mercy. In these hours of anguish, therefore, your children come to you as their hope.

We recognize your Queenship and ardently desire your triumph. We need a mother and a mother's heart. You are for us the luminous dawn that dissipates our darkness and points out the way to life. In your clemency obtain for us the courage and the confidence of which we have such need.

Most Holy and adorable Trinity, you who have crowned with

glory in heaven the Blessed Virgin Mary, Mother of the Savior, grant that all her children on earth may acknowledge her as their Sovereign Queen, that all hearts, homes, and nations may recognize her rights as Mother and as Queen. Amen.

ABOUT THE SHRINE

The Shrine of Mary Immaculate Queen is a humble and simple one located in the back of St. Pius X Church. There is a kneeler in front of the statue and a few vigil lights surrounding it. Approval to build the shrine was granted by the bishop of Joliet on May 13, 1974.

SHRINE INFORMATION

St. Pius X Church
1025 E. Madison Avenue
Lombard, IL 60148
(630) 627-4526

TOURIST INFORMATION

For specific information regarding hotels and restaurants, or explicit directions to the shrine, contact the rectory at the address above.

DIRECTIONS TO THE SHRINE

St. Pius X Church is located in Lombard, which is a western suburb of Chicago. Get on I-355 (North-South Tollway) and take the Roosevelt Road exit east. Then take Myers Westmore Road north. The church will be on the right, on the corner of Myers Westmore Road and Madison Avenue.

FOR FIRST-TIME PILGRIMS

The rosary, Benediction, and prayers are said each Wednesday evening from 8:00 until 9:00 P.M. in honor of Mary Immaculate Queen. The statue is located in the back of the church. If the church doors are locked, come to the rectory for the key.

OF SPECIAL INTEREST

Each evening the family should unite with all other families so consecrated by saying the prayer to Mary Immaculate Queen, for peace in the home, peace among our people, and peace in the world: "Mary Immaculate Queen, Triumph and Reign."

Monte Cassino Shrine

ST. MEINRAD ARCHABBEY
ST. MEINRAD, INDIANA

The place where you stand is holy ground.
EXODUS 3:5

In April 1853, two Benedictine monks of Einsiedeln Abbey in Switzerland arrived in Ferdinand, Indiana. Invited by the local bishop to train native clergy for the service of the growing German-speaking immigrant population, the monks were sent to choose a fitting site for a monastery and seminary. They found it in Spencer County, Indiana.

Despite the pioneering conditions in America, other monks of Einsiedeln soon followed. Before long, the priory was established under the patronage of Saint Meinrad, and students were sent to the fledgling seminary. The centuries-old tradition of Benedictine life accompanied by its special devotion to Our Lady of Einsiedeln was poised to take root in southern Indiana.

As a monk recites the rosary, hundreds of people follow prayerfully behind a statue of the Blessed Mother during a rosary procession at Monte Cassino Shrine.
(Monte Cassino Shrine)

From the beginning, monks and students discovered a favorite spot for hikes, picnics, and games on a wooded hill overlooking the Anderson Valley, about a mile from the monastery. The site was named Monte Cassino after the great abbey in Italy where Saint Benedict had renewed and inspired European monasticism in the sixth century. Sometime in 1857, a group of seminary students affixed a picture of the Immaculate Conception to an oak tree near the entrance to the grove. In the style of a wayside shrine, they carved a niche in the oaken trunk and protected the image with a crude roof of boards. Through such modest means, an invitation to pray was offered every passerby.

PILGRIM PRAYER TO OUR LADY OF MONTE CASSINO

Dearest Mother Mary, attracted to you by your goodness, sympathy, and motherliness, and also because of our needs, we have come as pilgrims to your shrine today. We love you, dearest Mother, and we pray that we may learn to love you more and more. We ask you to keep us always under your special protection, and to help us in all our needs. Please listen with love to the prayers and petitions of all who come to this shrine to seek your aid and to honor you. Also, obtain for each one of us through your powerful intercession with Jesus, your Son, all the graces we need to lead good lives and follow his teachings, especially his command to love one another. Amen.

ABOUT THE SHRINE

Shrines and holy places are found throughout the world. Some owe their fame to reports of apparitions, miracles, or revelations that have occurred there. Many are the historical sites of a divine call. In every case, a shrine represents the human yearning to experience what is holy—that is, to meet God. The enduring popularity of many shrines suggests that God responds to this yearning. God, indeed, meets the pilgrim through a deepening of faith, a stirring of emotion, a strengthening of commitment, a conversion of the heart, and in countless inexpressible ways.

The small Chapel of Monte Cassino, located on a forested hill near the Benedictine Archabbey and town of St. Meinrad, Indiana, makes no claim as a center of startling miracles or heavenly revelations. It owes its origin to a tradition—a very old tradition—of recognizing

God's miracles in ordinary things. It is a tradition that delights in praising the Virgin whose "let it be" has made God's grace shine forth everywhere in Christ.

The 125-year history of Monte Cassino does include, however, stories of physical healings, favors granted, and disasters averted. Undoubtedly, it includes countless personal miracles known only to God and the human heart. But above all, Monte Cassino is the local testament of an age-old pilgrimage: the pilgrimage of God's people, in the company of Mary, to the kingdom of her Son, Jesus Christ.

SHRINE INFORMATION

Fr. Louis Mulcahy, O.S.B.
Saint Meinrad Archabbey
St. Meinrad, IN 47577
(812) 357-6592 or (812) 357-6585

TOURIST INFORMATION

The Shrine of Monte Cassino is located in a rural area of southern Indiana and is accessible by car or bus. The Archabbey Guest House at Saint Meinrad Archabbey has accommodations for travelers that include twenty-five air-conditioned rooms furnished with twin beds, private bath, desk, and chairs. The facility, surrounded by beautiful grounds, includes a chapel, dining and conference rooms, and a lounge. Reservations can be made by calling (800) 581-6905 or (812) 357-6585. Rates are available for single- or double-occupancy rooms. Guaranteed room reservations can be made with a $20 nonrefundable deposit.

Meals are served three times each day in the Guest House Dining Room on the lower level. Reservations for meals are requested. For more information, call (812) 357-6495.

The Monastery Immaculate Conception, a monastery for Benedictine women, is located in the town of Ferdinand just six or seven miles away. The facilities there include a lovely grotto area that many visitors find attractive and refreshing. For more information, contact Karen Katafiasz, Director of Communication, at (812) 367-1411.

In addition, there are a number of hotel and motel accommodations throughout the area; for specific information, contact the Dubois

County Tourism Commission, 610 Main Street, Jasper, IN 47546, (812) 482-9115 or 1-800-ADVENTURE.

DIRECTIONS TO THE SHRINE

St. Meinrad is located in southern Indiana, about fifty miles west of Louisville.

FROM LOUISVILLE

Take I-64 west. * Go to exit 72 (Birdseye/Bristow) and exit left onto State Road 145. After you cross the interstate, the first intersection is SR 145 and SR 62. Take a right to head west. Go approximately eight miles. Saint Meinrad Archabbey is up off SR 62, just past the intersection of SR 62 and SR 545. (Monte Cassino has a blind entrance from this direction, on the north side of the road, and is about a mile east of Saint Meinrad Archabbey.)

FROM INDIANAPOLIS

Take I-65 south to I-64 west, then follow the directions at * just above.

FROM EVANSVILLE AND THE WEST

Get on I-64 east, exiting at the Ferdinand/Santa Claus exit 63. Take a right to get onto SR 162, heading south to the flashing light. At the flashing light, take a left to travel east on SR 62. Go about 4.5 miles, and the entrance to Saint Meinrad Archabbey will be on your right. Travel another mile or so on SR 62, and you will see the entrance to Monte Cassino on your left.

FOR FIRST-TIME PILGRIMS

The beauty of the shrine is its simplicity. On any given day, you can find someone in solitary prayer, either inside the shrine or somewhere on the grounds. The environment is perfect for encountering the Blessed Virgin one-on-one in prayer.

A visitor's guide to Saint Meinrad Archabbey provides basic information about the facilities at the archabbey, which operates Monte Cassino and is a draw of pilgrims in its own right. Visitors can take a tour of the buildings and grounds (including the beautifully renovated

Archabbey Church and its famous Our Lady of Einsiedeln statue), attend prayer or Mass with the monks, or shop for religious and inspirational products in the Abbey Gift Shop. Saint Meinrad Archabbey is about a mile southwest of the entrance to Monte Cassino Hill.

The shrine is open to the public during daytime hours every day of the year. Mass is held at the shrine on Saturday, Tuesday, and Thursday at 7:00 A.M. in the months of May and October. In the months of November through April, Mass is held only at 8:00 A.M. Mass is not offered at the shrine during the summer months. In addition, each Sunday during May and October a pilgrimage is offered at 2:00 P.M. Since the early 1930s these events of prayer, music, preaching, and rosary recitation have sometimes drawn more than a thousand people. These pilgrimages are quite an experience.

To share and promote the way to spiritual growth, the archabbey offers five types of retreat opportunities: weekend, midweek, group, guided, and private retreats. For more information about the retreat programs, contact Dr. Maurus Zoeller, O.S.B., Retreat Director, Archabbey Guest House, St. Meinrad, IN 47677, (812) 357-6585 or (800) 581-6905, fax (812) 357-6325.

OF SPECIAL INTEREST

The formal dedication of the Shrine of Monte Cassino occurred in May 1870. When smallpox threatened the region in the winter of 1872, the community was quick to turn to Our Lady of Monte Cassino. On December 1, the disease struck the village of St. Meinrad. Writing to a confrere in Einsiedeln, Dr. Isidor Hobi described the situation:

> *The smallpox broke out here before Christmas. In St. Meinrad, several children and two adults have succumbed to its ravages during the holiday, four persons had become infected here. Although we applied the best remedies and gave the patients the best possible care, the worst was to be feared. On January 4, the sick room was again occupied by four new patients, and in the dormitory others were ailing and awaiting dreadfully the first signs of the dreaded disease. Then we turned for help to Our Lady of Monte Cassino. On January 5, early in the morning, all the students who were able went on a pilgrimage to Monte*

Cassino where a solemn votive mass was offered. The pilgrimage was repeated on the last day of the novena (January 13) and, behold! On the evening of the first day only two were still in the infirmary. Since the beginning of the novena not a single case has broken out.

In gratitude for the Virgin's help in this crisis, it has been the custom since that time for representatives of Saint Meinrad's student body to make a pilgrimage to Monte Cassino each year on or near January 13.

$$+\|+\atop+\|+$$

Mother of Perpetual Help Shrine

ST. ALPHONSUS "ROCK" CHURCH
ST. LOUIS, MISSOURI

According to tradition, the first public veneration of the Icon of the Mother of Perpetual Help took place on March 27, 1499, in the old church of San Matteo in Rome, Italy. The icon remained at San Matteo, under the protection of the Augustinians, until January 19, 1886, when it was transferred to the Redemptorists by order of Pope Pius IX. The icon was restored to public veneration in the Church of St. Alphonsus (Sant' Alfonso), very close to the site of San Matteo in Rome, Italy.

The first copy of the Icon of Our Mother of Perpetual Help was installed at St. Mary's Church in Annapolis, Maryland, on August 15,

The Icon of Our Mother of Perpetual Help was installed at St. Alphonsus "Rock" Church in 1873. *(Anthony F. Chiffolo)*

1868. At the same time, other copies were enshrined in Ilchester, Maryland, at St. James (now Sacred Heart); St. Alphonsus in Baltimore, Maryland; Holy Redeemer in New York City; and St. Michael's Church in Chicago, Illinois. Five years later, on December 7, 1873, the Mother of Perpetual Help Shrine in St. Louis was solemnly erected and blessed.

PRAYER TO OUR MOTHER OF PERPETUAL HELP

O Mother of Perpetual Help, behold at your feet a wretched sinner who turns to you and puts all trust in you. Mother of mercy, have pity on me! I hear those who call you the refuge and the hope of sinners, be my refuge and be my hope! Help me for the love of Jesus Christ; hold out your hand to fallen sinners who commend and dedicate themselves forever to your service. Praise and thanks be to God, who in his great mercy has given me this trust in you, a sure pledge of my eternal salvation. Amen.

ABOUT THE SHRINE

At St. Alphonsus "Rock" Church, the first simple wooden shrine was replaced on July 2, 1893, with a shrine constructed of marble. The present shrine, dedicated and blessed on June 9, 1922, surpassed the beauty and the expense of the previous shrines. It is from this shrine that on June 11, 1922, the weekly Perpetual Help novena devotions were born and spread throughout the Catholic world.

SHRINE INFORMATION

Mother of Perpetual Help Shrine
St. Alphonsus "Rock" Church
1118 North Grand Boulevard
St. Louis, MO 63106
(314) 533-0304

TOURIST INFORMATION

Restaurant and hotel accommodations are readily available throughout the immediate area. Specific information can be obtained by writing to the above address.

DIRECTIONS TO THE SHRINE

St. Alphonsus "Rock" Church is located in north St. Louis and is easily accessible from any of the interstate highways that crisscross the city of St. Louis. Along Grand Boulevard you will also see Powell Symphony Hall and the Fox Theater. St. Alphonsus Church is just a few blocks north of these St. Louis landmarks, and most residents of St. Louis will easily be able to direct a pilgrim that may have difficulty finding the shrine.

FROM LAMBERT AIRPORT

The direct route is to travel east on I-70, exit south on Grand Boulevard, and proceed south for approximately two miles.

FROM THE WEST

St. Alphonsus "Rock" Church is off the Grand Boulevard exit of I-44. Proceed north on Grand for approximately two miles.

FROM THE EAST

Proceed north on Grand Boulevard from I-44, I-40, or I-64.

FOR FIRST-TIME PILGRIMS

St. Alphonsus "Rock" Church, the church in which the shrine is located, is a vibrant inner-city, African-American parish. Although the church has retained the architectural splendor of a different age, it is a showcase for African-American liturgy, preaching, song, and worship. The "sacred space" of the church is reflective of the rich traditions of the African-American community.

Visitors to Mother of Perpetual Help Shrine will not want to miss the weekly devotions, which are scheduled on Tuesdays at 7:00 A.M. and 10:30 A.M. and Saturdays at 8:00 A.M. (prayers before Mass). In addition, it is worth making time to attend either the 8:30 A.M. or the 11:00 A.M. Sunday Mass. The church is always filled, and it is wise to plan on arriving at least thirty minutes ahead of schedule in order to get a seat. It is also important to plan on Mass lasting approximately two hours. Sunday liturgy at the "Rock" Church is an experience of grace and worship that is unsurpassed and memorable!

OF SPECIAL INTEREST

Just a few blocks south of St. Alphonsus Church is the college church of St. Francis Xavier, at St. Louis University. A vibrant worshiping community, it is also the original home of the "St. Louis Jesuits," well known for their songs that are featured in most Catholic hymnals. In addition, the Church of St. Francis Xavier is the home of a statue of Mary that commemorates the favorable intercession of the Blessed Mother during the plague of 1849. According to the annals of the city of St. Louis, approximately six thousand of the seventy thousand inhabitants of the city had perished in the cholera epidemic during the months of May and June. At St. Louis University (at that time located on Ninth and Washington) Fr. Isadore J. Boudreaux, S.J., urged the students to pray for Mary's protection. Evidently, their prayers were heard, as witnessed by the plaque that was secured below the statue of Mary in the college chapel. The plaque, as translated from the Latin, tells the story:

> In memory of the favor bestowed through the intercession of Mary, A.D. 1849, while the pestilence was raging in this city and, in the space of a few months, six thousand citizens perished, the rector, professors, and students of this University, finding themselves in imminent danger of death, prayed to Mary, Mother of God and of men, and bound themselves by a vow to place a silver crown upon her statue if every member of the University was preserved from infection. This great confidence in the Mother of God pleased her Divine Son, for the devastating scourge through the intercession of Mary was not permitted to enter the walls of the University; and to the admiration of the entire city, not even one of the more than two hundred resident students was affected by the plague.

According to the records of the college church, the silver crown mentioned was placed upon the statue's head every year until 1969, when the practice was ended. In addition, due to the renovation of the church in 1990, the statue of Our Lady was moved to the Chapel of Our Lady, which is the lower church; the entrance is clearly marked on Grand Boulevard. Daily Mass is offered in the chapel at 7:15 A.M., noon, and 5:15 P.M., but it is always good to call for exact Mass times. The telephone number is (314) 977-7300.

National Shrine of Mary, Help of Christians

HUBERTUS, WISCONSIN

Many people wonder why the Catholic Church has such great reverence for Mary. The simple reason is that she is the Mother of our Lord and Savior Jesus Christ, and since we honor our own mothers, all the more reason to honor his.

The place known as Holy Hill is dedicated to Mary's honor under the title Mary, Help of Christians. The life-size statue of Our Lady of Holy Hill is a beautiful representation of Mary presenting her Son to the world. This masterpiece was made in Munich, Germany, and brought to America by the Pustet firm for the Philadelphia World's Fair in 1876. A devout Wisconsin man purchased the statue for Holy Hill,

Often called "Holy Hill," the National Shrine of Mary, Help of Christians offers an unparalleled glimpse of its dramatic rural Wisconsin surroundings. *(Anthony F. Chiffolo)*

but for practical reasons it was first taken to St. Hubert's Parish in Hubertus, where it remained for two years. On July 1, 1878, eighteen young barefoot women, dressed in white robes with blue ribbons, carried the statue from St. Hubert's in Hubertus seven miles to the log chapel at the top of Holy Hill. The women were escorted by an entourage of one hundred men on horseback, many priests, and delegates from all over the state. These dedicated pilgrims filled the air with prayers and songs as they processed to their goal.

PRAYER TO MARY, HELP OF CHRISTIANS

Most Holy and Immaculate Virgin, Help of Christians, we place ourselves under your motherly protection. Throughout the Church's history you have helped Christians in times of trial, temptation, and danger. Time and time again you have proven to be the Refuge of sinners, the Hope of the hopeless, the Consoler of the afflicted, and the Comforter of the dying. We promise to be faithful disciples of Jesus Christ, your Son, to proclaim his Good News of God's love for all people, and to work for peace and justice in our world. With faith in your intercession, we pray for the Church, for our family and friends, for the poor and abandoned, and all the dying. Grant, O Mary, Help of Christians, the graces of which we stand in need. (Mention your intentions.) May we serve Jesus with fidelity and love until death. Help us and our loved ones to attain the boundless joy of being forever with our Father in heaven. Amen.

ABOUT THE SHRINE

The ivory colored and gold-leaf statue of Our Lady of Holy Hill stands in the beautiful forty-by-fifty-foot shrine chapel to the right of the sanctuary in the upper church. Below the base of the statue is an elegant bouquet of hand-beaten bronze roses covered with simulated ruby-studded rosettes strung together by a rope of simulated sapphires. The statue is set against a circular wall of pink-veined Kasota marble.

Reverence for Mary is further expressed in a set of beautiful stained-glass windows illustrating the Hail, Holy Queen, and in the stained-glass windows in the upper church portraying Mary's life.

Holy Hill also offers pilgrims a chance to walk along the half mile outdoor Way of the Cross with fourteen groups of life-size sculptures representing the passion of Jesus. Others may pray at the Lourdes Grotto or stroll around four hundred wooded acres crossed by Wisconsin's Ice-Age Trail. During summer and fall, thousands climb 178 steps to the top of the observation tower inside one of the church spires for an unparalleled glimpse of the dramatic rural surroundings and the skyline of Milwaukee on the horizon.

SHRINE INFORMATION

Holy Hill
National Shrine of Mary, Help of Christians
Discalced Carmelite Friars
1525 Carmel Road
Hubertus, WI 53033-9407
(414) 628-1838

TOURIST INFORMATION

For specific information regarding food and lodging, call the monastery office. At Holy Hill, simple but comfortable guest rooms and group retreat facilities are available with advance reservations at a reasonable cost. The Old Monastery Inn Cafeteria produces nourishing and tasty meals as well as simple snacks. The cafeteria is open weekends year-round, including Sunday brunch, and daily from June 1 until October 31. The shrine is handicapped accessible to the church and the rest rooms. A large gift shop features books and pamphlets, audio- and videotapes, rosaries and crucifixes, and candles and other religious articles.

DIRECTIONS TO THE SHRINE

Holy Hill is located 110 miles north of Chicago, 70 miles east of Madison, 30 miles northwest of Milwaukee, and 5 miles south of Hartford.

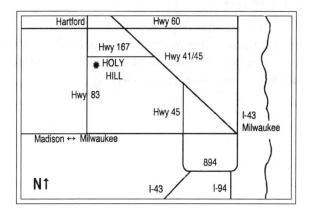

FROM CHICAGO, MILWAUKEE, AND THE SOUTH

Take I-94 north to I-894; go west and north on I-894. Continue north on US Hwy. 45 and 41 to the State Hwy. 167 exit. Go west on State Hwy. 167 approximately seven miles to the Holy Hill entrance.

FROM MADISON AND THE WEST

Take I-94 east to the State Hwy. 83 exit; go north on State Hwy. 83 to State Hwy. 167. Go east on State Hwy. 167 approximately two miles to the Holy Hill entrance.

FROM FOND DU LAC AND THE NORTH

Take US Hwy. 41 south to the State Hwy. 167 exit; go west on State Hwy. 167 approximately seven miles to the Holy Hill entrance.

FOR FIRST-TIME PILGRIMS

The Discalced Carmelite Friars and other staff at Holy Hill welcome visits by individuals and groups year-round. For special arrangements, simply contact the Monastery Office.

There is a full weekend Mass schedule along with Marian devotions and daily religious services. The sacrament of reconciliation, traditionally associated with shrines, is readily available for those desiring it. Special seasonal events occur throughout the year, including a live Nativity, uplifting religious concerts, and a popular arts and crafts fair.

OF SPECIAL INTEREST

Opening off the main body of the church is the Shrine Chapel with its inspiring statue of Mary presenting her Son to the world. Crutches and other mementos line one wall of the entrance, evidence of the faith of those who have sought aid in this holy place.

National Shrine of Our Lady of Lebanon
NORTH JACKSON, OHIO

The National Shrine of Our Lady of Lebanon in North Jackson, Ohio, is a replica of a shrine located in Harissa, Lebanon. Our Lady of Lebanon is a unique title for our Blessed Mother, as it is a name that can be found in the Bible. The title *Lebanon,* a name of a land in the Middle East—the Holy Lands—was always a special image depicting her as a bride and queen of the Father. This quotation is engraved at the base of the Statue of Our Lady of Lebanon and is taken from the Song of Songs, chapter four:

> *Come from Lebanon, my bride,*
> *Come from Lebanon, come…*
> *and the fragrance of your garments*
> *is the fragrance of Lebanon.*

PRAYER TO THE MOTHER OF GOD

O immaculate and pure Virgin Mary, Mother of God, Queen of the Universe, our own good Lady; you are above all the saints, the only hope of the patriarchs, and the joy of all the saints. Through you we have been reconciled with our God. You are the only advocate of sinners, and the secure haven of those who are sailing on the sea of this life. O great Princess, Mother of God, cover us with the wings of your mercy and pity us. We hope only in you, O most pure Virgin.

SAINT EPHREM

ABOUT THE SHRINE

The Shrine of Our Lady of Lebanon was five years in planning and one year in construction. The tower stands 50 feet high and weighs 3,700 tons. The statue of Our Lady is of solid pink granite from North Carolina and stands 12 feet tall, with a granite pedestal 4.5 feet high.

There are sixty-four steps to the top—one for each prayer of the rosary.

On July 20, 1965, the statue of the Virgin Mary was placed atop the tower. As the statue was put in place, a large cloud turned all the brilliant shades of the rainbow. This was interpreted as a sign that the Blessed Virgin was smiling on the project.

The National Shrine of Our Lady of Lebanon is a replica of a shrine located in Harissa, Lebanon.
(National Shrine of Our Lady of Lebanon)

SHRINE INFORMATION

National Shrine of Our Lady of Lebanon
2759 North Lipkey Road
North Jackson, OH 44451
(330) 538-3351

TOURIST INFORMATION

There are a number of restaurant facilities in the nearby areas; however, groups with prior reservations may arrange for home-cooked meals available from breakfast, sandwich, or dinner menus. Overnight accommodations can be arranged at the following motels/hotels:

- Best Western Meander Inn: 870 N. Canfield Road, Youngstown, OH 44515, (800) 528-1234
- Quality Inn of Youngstown: 1051 N. Canfield-Niles Road, Youngstown, OH 44515, (216) 793-9851
- Budget Luxury Inn: 5425 Clarkins Drive, Youngstown, OH 44515, (216) 793-9806
- Super 8 Motel: 5280 Seventy-Six Drive, Youngstown, OH 44515, (800) 800-8000

DIRECTIONS TO THE SHRINE

The National Shrine of Our Lady of Lebanon, located in North Jackson, is less than ten miles west of Youngstown. Pilgrims arriving from the east or west on I-80 (in Ohio or Pennsylvania) should exit at the intersection of I-80 and Rte. 46 just west of Youngstown. Go south on Rte. 46 for two miles to Mahoning Avenue (Rte. 18) and turn right (west). Go three miles on Mahoning Avenue to Lipkey Road and turn right (north). Go two miles on Lipkey Road to the shrine on the right.

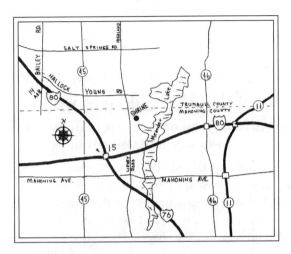

FOR FIRST-TIME PILGRIMS

The Shrine of Our Lady of Lebanon, located on a peaceful, pastoral eighty-acre setting, is open year-round daily from 9:00 A.M. to 5:00 P.M. It is completely handicapped accessible. Everything is available indoors if weather does not allow for outdoor activities. Pilgrims are encouraged to walk the meditation trail dedicated to the Holy Family or visit the outdoor Stations of the Cross. Mass is celebrated daily, preceded by the rosary on weekdays. Devotion to Our Lady of Lebanon and the blessing with the relic of Saint Sharbel is every Wednesday morning at 8:00 A.M.

OF SPECIAL INTEREST

The Diocese of St. Maron in the United States operates the Shrine of Our Lady of Lebanon. The Maronites have their origins in ancient Syria, a country that embraced many cultures. Faced with the destruction of their faith during the Arab invasions, the Maronites migrated and settled in the mountains of Lebanon. During the centuries to follow, the Maronites carried their faith to Mexico, Africa, Australia, and

North and South America as they became citizens of many nations. They are deeply devoted to Mary, the Mother of the Light, hailing her strength and fidelity in the title "Cedar of Lebanon."

National Shrine of Our Lady of the Miraculous Medal

THE ASSOCIATION OF THE MIRACULOUS MEDAL
PERRYVILLE, MISSOURI

The Miraculous Medal and the prayer inscribed upon it originated in heaven with the Blessed Mother herself. On the night of July 18, 1839, Sr. Catherine Labouré, a novice of the Daughters of Charity at their mother house in Paris, was aroused from sleep by her guardian angel and summoned to the chapel. There, one of her most ardent

The National Shrine of Our Lady of the Miraculous Medal commemorates the apparition of the Blessed Mother to Saint Catherine Labouré, who received the Miraculous Medal. *(National Shrine of Our Lady of the Miraculous Medal)*

desires was fulfilled—she saw the Blessed Mother. Seated on the left side of the sanctuary, Mary summoned Catherine to her and told her that she had been chosen for a special mission. France would fall upon evil days and the whole world would be in sorrow. "But come to the foot of this altar," said the Holy Mother. "There graces shall be showered upon you and upon all those who shall ask for them, rich or poor."

Mary again appeared to her humble servant on November 27, and this time gave to her the design of the medal she wished to have made and the prayer she would have her children say to her: "O Mary conceived without sin, pray for us who have recourse to thee!" A third apparition was granted to Catherine in December.

Mary's design was carried out, and the medals were made as we know them today. The Blessed Virgin stands on a half-globe, her foot crushing the head of the serpent and luminous rays issuing from her extended hands, in symbol of the graces she obtains for those who ask for them. Surrounding this image is the invocation "O Mary conceived without sin, pray for us who have recourse to thee!" The reverse of the medals bears the letter *M* surmounted by a cross, having a bar at its base, and beneath this monogram of Mary are the hearts of Jesus, surrounded with a crown of thorns, and of Mary, transpierced with a sword.

From France, the devotion to the medal spread all over the world, and the medal came to be known as miraculous because of the wonderful cures, both of soul and body, wrought through it. From the beginning, the Church has sanctioned this devotion to the Immaculate Conception of the Blessed Virgin Mary by means of the Miraculous Medal, and various popes have endowed it with many indulgences. Catherine was beatified by Pope Pius XI on May 28, 1933, and on July 27, 1947, she was canonized by his successor, our Holy Father Pope Pius XII.

Today it has been more than 130 years since Our Lady appeared to Saint Catherine Labouré and gave her the Miraculous Medal. During this time countless millions of medals have been distributed, and "Mary's Prayer in Metal Form" has brought and still brings many wonderful favors to those who pray to her with confidence.

PRAYER TO OUR LADY OF THE MIRACULOUS MEDAL

O Virgin Mother of God, Mary Immaculate, we dedicate and consecrate ourselves to you under the title of Our Lady of the Miraculous Medal. May this medal be for each one of us a sure sign of your affection for us and a constant reminder of our duties toward you. Ever while wearing it, may we be blessed by your loving protection and preserved in the grace of your Son. O Most powerful Virgin, Mother of our Savior, keep us close to you every moment of our lives. Obtain for us, your children, the grace of a happy death; so that, in union with you, we may enjoy the bliss of heaven forever. Amen.

ABOUT THE SHRINE

The Shrine of Our Lady of the Miraculous Medal, built in 1928 by the Promoters of the Miraculous Medal Association, replaced the Chapel of St. Vincent in St. Mary's of the Barrens Church in Perryville, Missouri. The new shrine is a replica of the church sanctuary and has been a source of inspiration and a center of devotion for Our Lady of the Miraculous Medal.

Visitors to the shrine are encouraged to place their petitions in the marble urn in the center of the shrine sanctuary. Petitions are remembered in the daily Mass at the shrine.

SHRINE INFORMATION

The Association of the Miraculous Medal
1811 West Saint Joseph Street
Perryville, MO 63775
(573) 547-8344

TOURIST INFORMATION

Lodging for visitors to the shrine is available at the Best Western Colonial Inn and the Budget Host Inn located nearby. There are as well a number of restaurants.

DIRECTIONS TO THE SHRINE

The National Shrine of Our Lady of the Miraculous Medal is eighty miles south of St. Louis, Missouri, off I-55. To reach the shrine, exit at the junction of I-55 and State Hwy. 51, taking Hwy. 51 north. At the junction with State Road T (St. Joseph Street), turn left. The shrine is within a quarter mile of this junction. If approaching from the east (Illinois), follow State

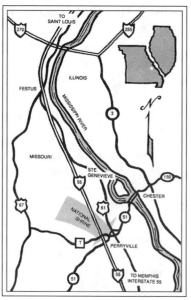

Hwy. 51 around Perryville, Missouri, to the junction with State Road T (St. Joseph Street).

FOR FIRST-TIME PILGRIMS

First-time pilgrims to the shrine are encouraged to participate in Mass, receive a guided tour of the shrine and museums, and spend time on the grounds in prayer and meditation. Spring and fall are beautiful at the shrine. Mass is celebrated daily at 8:00 A.M. and on Sunday at 11:00 A.M. Confessions and the novena service are scheduled every Monday at 7:15 P.M. (after Mass). The annual May Procession is on the first Sunday of May at 3:30 P.M., and the annual Christmas novena is December 16–24 at 7:30 in the evening.

OF SPECIAL INTEREST

The many favors that God has granted through the intercession of Mary, by means of her Miraculous Medal, should not be the occasion of superstition. The Miraculous Medal does not possess of itself the power to procure good things for us or to avert evil. It is not a "good luck" charm or an amulet. It is simply a sacramental approved by the Church. It can be called a prayer in metal form, and its purpose is exactly the same as that of the prayers we say in invoking the aid of the Mother of God. Mary herself designed this miraculous badge of her faithful clients and sanctioned its devout use. The Church blesses it with solemn prayer and imposes it upon the shoulders of the wearer, who according to Mary's promise will thereby receive "great graces."

✠

National Shrine of Our Lady of Providence

SISTERS OF PROVIDENCE
SAINT MARY-OF-THE WOODS, INDIANA

The Sisters of Providence of Saint Mary-of-the-Woods, Indiana, established the National Shrine of Our Lady of Providence in May 1925. Devotion to Mary under the title of Our Lady of Providence began with the first shrine dedicated to her in the Church of San Carlo ai Catinari in Italy in 1732. The artist Scipione Pulzone, known as Gaetano, created the original painting of Our Lady of Providence. Msgr. A. J. Rawlinson, chaplain of the Sisters of Providence, learned of the history of the painting and of the numerous miracles associated with the shrine in the Church of San Carlo and immediately recognized its significance for the Sisters of Providence. As a result, a shrine of Our Lady of Providence was erected in the corridor outside the Blessed Sacrament Chapel and the Church of the Immaculate Conception at Providence Center and is officially recognized by Rome as a national shrine. Pilgrims from throughout the United States visit the National Shrine of Our Lady of Providence. Under the title Queen of the Home, she is a special source of comfort and inspiration for families.

The National Shrine of Our Lady of Providence features a reproduction of the famous *Mother and Child* painting by Gaetano, and pilgrims who pray before her invoke her as "Queen of the Home," especially on behalf of families. *(National Shrine of Our Lady of Providence)*

PRAYER OF INTERCESSION THROUGH MARY, QUEEN OF THE HOME

O God, whose ever-watchful providence rules all things, we humbly implore you, through the prayer of the Blessed Virgin Mary, Mother of your Son, to remove from us whatever is harmful and to bestow on us only that which will be helpful. We ask this through Jesus Christ, your Son, who lives and reigns with you and the Holy Spirit, one God, forever and ever. Amen.

ABOUT THE SHRINE

The focus of the Shrine of Our Lady of Providence is the strengthening of families. At the center of the shrine is the reproduction of the famous *Mother and Child* painting by Gaetano. Our Lady lovingly embraces her infant son, Jesus, in the picture, and those who pray before her invoke her as "Queen of the Home," especially on behalf of families.

In addition to the shrine, the grounds also include the Immaculate Conception Grotto, the Lady of Fátima Shrine, the large Our Lady of Lourdes Grotto beautifully surrounded by flowers and trees, and an outdoor Stations of the Cross.

SHRINE INFORMATION

The Shrine
Providence Center
1 Sisters of Providence
Saint Mary-of-the-Woods, IN 47876-1092
(812) 535-3131, ext. 145
fax: (812) 535-3675

TOURIST INFORMATION

Restaurant and hotel accommodations are available in the Terre Haute area. Possibilities include

- Holiday Inn of Terre Haute: (812) 232-6081
- Larry Bird's Boston Connection: (812) 235-3333
- Signature Inn: (812) 238-1461

DIRECTIONS TO THE SHRINE

Saint Mary-of-the-Woods is 77 miles west of Indianapolis, 113 miles north of Evansville, 190 miles south of Chicago, and just 4.5 miles northwest of downtown Terre Haute. Providence Center is easily accessible from I-70.

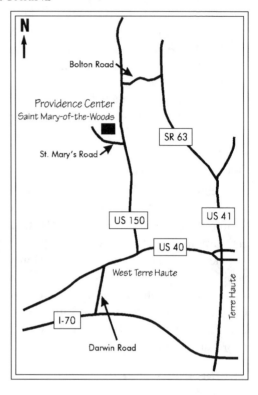

FROM TERRE HAUTE

At the Vigo County Courthouse, turn west onto US 40. Cross the bridge and proceed to the first stoplight in West Terre Haute, the intersection of US 40 and US 150. Turn right on US 150. * Proceed approximately two miles to St. Mary's Road and the sign for Saint Mary-of-the-Woods College. Turn left onto St. Mary's Road. ** Proceed to the main entrance (the second gate). Turn right and proceed to the end of the avenue; go right at the fountain. Providence Center and parking are directly north of the fountain.

FROM I-70

Coming from either direction, take exit 3. Proceed north on Darwin Road to US 40. Turn right on US 40 and proceed to US 150 in West Terre Haute. Turn left on US 150. Follow the directions at * just above.

FROM THE NORTH ON SR 63

Turn right on Bolton Road (approximately nine miles south of Clinton, Indiana). Proceed to US 150 and turn left. Follow US 150 to

St. Mary's Road (do not turn at SMW School of Equine Studies). Turn right onto St. Mary's Road. Follow the directions at ** above.

FOR FIRST-TIME PILGRIMS

In addition to visiting the shrine, pilgrims are also welcome to visit the Church of the Immaculate Conception. Built before the turn of the century, the church is the place of daily worship for more than three hundred sisters who live at Saint Mary-of-the-Woods. Visitors are invited to celebrate the Eucharistic liturgy with the Sisters of Providence Monday through Saturday at 11:30 A.M. and on Sunday at 10:00 A.M.

OF SPECIAL INTEREST

Venerable Mother Theodore Guerin, foundress of the Sisters of Providence of Saint Mary-of-the-Woods, was a woman of immeasurable faith with a profound devotion to Mary, the Mother of Jesus. Mother Theodore led her community with strength and confidence in prayer. While sailing to France in savage storms that threatened the lives of everyone aboard ship, Mother Theodore committed their safety to the protection of the Blessed Mother and was returned safely to the United States. She wrote in her journal, "What strength the soul draws from prayer! In the midst of a storm, how sweet is the calm it finds in the Heart of Jesus. But what comfort is there for those who do not pray?"

National Shrine of Our Lady of the Snows

MISSIONARY OBLATES OF MARY IMMACULATE
BELLEVILLE, ILLINOIS

Devotion to the Mother of Jesus under a particular title is usually linked to one of Mary's privileges (Immaculate Conception, Assumption) or qualities (Mother of Mercy, Queen of Peace) or to one of her apparitions (Our Lady of Lourdes, Our Lady of Guadalupe). Devotion to Mary under the title of Our Lady of the Snows falls into a different category, however, and dates from A.D. 352.

According to legend, on the hot sultry night of August 4 of that year, Our Lady appeared to a childless, wealthy Roman couple in a dream. She expressed a wish that a church be built in her honor in Rome. She told them that the site for the church would be covered with a blanket of snow. On this same night, she also appeared to Pope Liberius in a dream, telling him of her desire.

On the morning of August 5, the citizens of Rome awoke to an astonishing sight. The Esquiline Hill was covered with snow, even though the weather was extremely warm. All

The Main Shrine at Our Lady of the Snows commemorates Mary's miraculous message to a wealthy Roman couple in A.D. 352. *(Anthony F. Chiffolo)*

Rome proclaimed the summer snow a miracle, and the couple accepted this as a sign that they were to use their wealth to help build the church.

In time, the magnificent Basilica of St. Mary Major was built on this site. Restored and refurbished several times, the basilica still stands today as the seat of devotion to Our Lady of the Snows. At the National Shrine of Our Lady of the Snows in Belleville, Illinois, Our Lady is honored, not so much because of the legend, but because of her special role in a Church that is, by its very nature, missionary.

OUR LADY OF THE SNOW

The Romans tell a legend rare,
A quaintly sweet and graceful story,
How first the site was chosen, where
Is built the temple grandly fair....

There dwelt in Rome a noble pair—
(When faith ruled hearts with stronger power)

Vast wealth was theirs that had no heir—
No spendthrift son to waste his share,
No daughter yearning for her dower.

And so, for Him whose Hand bestowed
Their golden store in bounteous measure,
They vowed to build a fair abode,
And thus, where "moth could not corrode,"
To shrine rare wealth of heavenly treasure.

But long they sought a fitting site
Whereon to build the dome of splendor,
Praying meanwhile, Our Lady bright,
In gracious vision of the night
To lend her aid, benign and tender.

The prayer of trusting Faith was heard—
Heaven on their hearts' sincere petition
The boon of blessing reply conferred—
And to Our Lady's gracious word
Glad heed they gave, and wise submission.
Ave Maria!

ABOUT THE SHRINE

In an effort to meet the human and spiritual needs of people in today's world, the National Shrine of Our Lady of the Snows, through its hospitality and programs, invites people to experience the healing message of God's boundless love and calls upon them to carry that message to others. Above all else, the shrine is designed to be more than just a beautiful place to visit. The shrine is a place for people. To meet the needs of its thousands of visitors annually, the shrine has established an extensive spiritual ministry that strives to bring its visitors and all people to a greater awareness of the presence of Christ in their lives. Highlights of the shrine include

- The Main Shrine: The Main Shrine is nestled in a gentle valley surrounded by trees and flowers. The shrine amphitheater's 2,400 seats and grassy slopes can accommodate large crowds for special liturgies and events. The Christ the King Chapel, Mary Chapel, and Rosary Courts are located in the Main Shrine area.

- The Way of the Cross: The Way of the Cross begins in a serene setting amidst a grove of evergreens and pines. Each station with meditations consists of detailed full-color groupings of Christ, Mary, and others associated with Christ's journey to Calvary.
- Resurrection Garden: The Resurrection Garden is located near the end of the Way of the Cross to symbolize Christ's victory over sin and death. The cave exterior resembles a common stone. The interior simulates a cut geode. A continuous flame burns as a symbol of the everlasting life that Christ promised.
- Lourdes Grotto: The Lourdes Grotto, a replica of the famed grotto in Lourdes, France, is located in a beautiful wooded area of the shrine. From the day of completion, it has been a favorite devotional site for visiting pilgrims.
- Annunciation Garden: The Annunciation Garden, standing majestically on the hill overlooking the amphitheater, features a larger-than-life sculpture of the Annunciation scene. The tolling of four large bells, located above a reflecting pool, dramatically marks each hour. Fr. Edwin J. Guild, O.M.I., the shrine founder, is buried in front of the Annunciation sculpture, and engraved on the tombstone is his greeting to people coming to the Shrine: "God love you for visiting Our Lady's Shrine."
- Mother's Prayer Walk: The Mother's Prayer Walk, adjacent to the Annunciation Garden, is a tribute to mothers everywhere. In this beautiful, inspiring location, memorial plaques honor individual mothers. Landscaped flower gardens, which brighten the area throughout the season, surround the memorial walkway.
- Father's Memorial Wall: The Memorial Wall honors Jesus, the Carpenter, and all fathers. It is at the top of a wooded walkway winding down a hillside to the Lourdes Grotto. Memorials are found on the walls at the entrance.
- The Edwin J. Guild Center: *The Journey,* one of the most impressive devotional experiences at the shrine, is in the Edwin J. Guild Center, named after the founder of the shrine. A sight-and-sound experience, *The Journey* leads people on a

pilgrimage through creation, the Fall, and humanity's search for meaning and redemption.

- Church of Our Lady of the Snows: The Church of Our Lady of the Snows is the newest addition at the shrine. It enhances the liturgies and programs that are part of the shrine's ministry.
- Agony Garden: The Agony Garden, sitting in a dense grove of trees, is a perfect place for visitors to pray and reflect in quiet solitude. The area is enhanced by tall maple and cottonwood trees, unfolding its special seasonal beauty.

SHRINE INFORMATION

National Shrine of Our Lady of the Snows
442 South De Mazenod Drive
Belleville, IL 62223-1094
(618) 397-6700 or (314) 241-3400
fax: (618) 398-6549

TOURIST INFORMATION

The Shrine of Our Lady of the Snows is open every day of the year to people of all faiths and denominations. Admission is free. Mass is celebrated daily at various times, with the sacrament of reconciliation available thirty minutes before each Mass or upon request. The St. Joseph's Visitors Center, the Dr. Tom Dooley Center, and the Shrine Motel provide the necessary accommodations for pilgrims. Visitors can obtain information on programs and events, view a shrine video or slide presentation, shop for a special remembrance at the gift shop, and dine in the shrine restaurant. Conferences and meeting rooms are available in both the Visitors and Dooley Centers.

A truly spiritual way to visit the shrine is through a group pilgrimage. With the help of the shrine's pilgrimage director and pilgrimage leaders throughout the United States, special conferences, discussions, and prayer services are available for groups visiting the shrine.

The AAA-rated Shrine Motel provides comfortable accommodations at a modest price. A complimentary continental breakfast is served daily. Group rates and rooms for persons with disabilities are available upon request. The shrine gift shop, one of the largest in the St. Louis metro area, has gifts for all ages and occasions. An extensive book section covers a wide variety of interests.

While visiting the shrine, pilgrims are encouraged to walk, drive, or take a complimentary tram tour of the grounds.

DIRECTIONS TO THE SHRINE

The National Shrine of Our Lady of the Snows, the largest outdoor shrine in the United States, is located on Hwy. 15, just twenty minutes from the Gateway Arch in downtown St. Louis, Missouri.

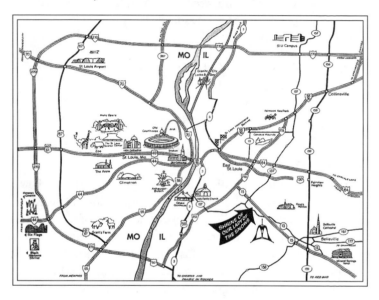

FROM ST. LOUIS

Take I-70, I-40, I-44, or I-55 toward Illinois. As you approach the Mississippi River, follow the signs for Illinois—these will take you across the river on I-55/I-70. Once across the river, take the St. Clair Avenue/I-64 exit. Stay on I-64 to I-255, then take I-255 south until you reach Illinois Rte. 15 east (exit 17A). Exit at 15 east and the shrine will be two miles on the right.

FROM CHICAGO AND SPRINGFIELD

Take I-55 south, then take the exit off the interstate marked "157-Caseyville-Edwardsville." Turn right onto Illinois 157 south. Continue on 157 south for about ten miles to Illinois Rte. 15. Turn left onto Rte. 15. The shrine will be on your right at the top of the hill.

FOR FIRST-TIME PILGRIMS

First-time pilgrims to the Shrine of Our Lady of the Snows should stop first at the St. Joseph's Visitors Center. Inside the center is a theater describing the shrine and all it has to offer. There is also a restaurant and gift shop there. The shrine is accessible to handicapped persons. There are free guided open-air trams that run from April through October. The shrine is open every day of the year from 8:00 A.M. to 8:00 P.M.

OF SPECIAL INTEREST

Located at the far end of the St. Joseph's Visitors Center, the Dr. Tom Dooley Center houses the shrine's Pastoral Team and several outreach programs. Meeting and conference rooms for many of the shrine's activities are found in the Dooley Center.

The building is dedicated to the late Dr. Tom Dooley, who worked with the Oblates in Southeast Asia in the 1950s. Dr. Dooley achieved world recognition for his work on behalf of the poor. Together, Dr. Dooley and the Oblate missionaries affected the lives of thousands of needy people and refugees in Laos, Cambodia, Vietnam, and other Southeast Asian nations. In 1958 Dr. Dooley was made an Honorary Oblate because of his continuing support of the Oblates' missionary work.

Two of the shrine's outreach programs include the Radio Information Service, a closed-circuit radio reading service that broadcasts exclusively to persons with visual and physical disabilities within a fifty-mile radius of the shrine, and the Victorious Missionaries, a ministry for persons with disabilities, facilitated by persons with disabilities.

Our Lady of Consolation

ST. AUGUSTINE CHURCH
LEOPOLD, INDIANA

Devotion to Our Lady of Consolation began in the early seventeenth century in Luxembourg, the capital of a country of the same name once known for its national devotion to Mary, Consoler of the Afflicted, when one of the worst catastrophes of the age struck: the bubonic plague. The death toll was so staggering that, as one historian wrote, "neither grave diggers nor cemeteries could be found adequate to bury the many dead." In their anguish and fear, the people fervently invoked the aid of Mary, Consoler of the Afflicted.

At that time a chapel was being built outside the city of Luxembourg. The priest in charge of the building of the chapel, Father Brodquart, contracted the disease himself. While he lay near death, he made a vow to Our Blessed Mother that, if he were spared and allowed to finish the work, he would dedicate the chapel to Our Lady of Consolation. His fever fell; he recovered and resumed building the chapel. On May 10, 1628, the small chapel was dedicated to Mary, Consoler of the Afflicted, and a statue was placed on the chapel altar. Many and varied cures of sickness were soon attributed to the prayers offered at the shrine. Some of these cures have been recognized by the Catholic Church as bona fide miracles.

PRAYER TO OUR LADY OF CONSOLATION

Immaculate Virgin Mary, Mother of God and our most compassionate Mother, we present ourselves in your sight in all humility, and with full confidence we implore you for your maternal patronage. You are the comforter of the afflicted, and to you constant recourse is had by the sorrowful in their afflictions, the sick in their maladies, the dying in their agony, and the poor in their strained circumstances; and from you they all receive consolation and strength. Comfort our spirits, troubled and afflicted in

*the midst of many dangers that threaten us. This we ask through
the immense joy that filled our pure soul in the glorious Resurrection of your Divine Son. Amen.*

ABOUT THE SHRINE

The story of the shrine in Leopold, Indiana, begins on September
19, 1863, at the Battle of Chimauga (a creek in Georgia) during the
Civil War. The Union forces were defeated, and many prisoners were
taken. They were sent to the prison at Andersonville, Georgia. This
prison became known as "Maniac's Nightmare" because of the brutal
treatment the prisoners received. More than fourteen thousand Northern soldiers died there from starvation and disease, from maulings by
bloodhounds, and from beatings by their crazed and starved fellow
prisoners. At war's end, the officer in charge of the camp, Capt. Henry
Wirtz, was tried by a military court and sentenced to hang.

Among the Andersonville prisoners were three young men from
Perry County, Indiana, members of St. Augustine Church in Leopold.
They were Lamber Rogier, Henry Devillez, and Isidore Navlaux. Being
men of faith, they turned to prayer and Our Blessed Mother for help
and consolation. Henry Devillez had come to the States from Belgium
as a boy of fourteen, and he remembered the Shrine of Our Lady of
Consolation in the Duchy of Luxembourg. In their present affliction,
the three men made a vow that, if they survived prison, one of them
would return to their native land of Belgium and have a replica of the
statue made and bring it back to St. Augustine Church.

After almost eleven months as prisoners, they were freed. After a
number of hardships, they reached their homes in Perry County and
set about finding a way to fulfill their vow. John P. George, who lived in
Troy, Indiana, made frequent trips back to Belgium. Aware of this, Lam-
bert Rogier contacted Mr. George and traveled with him to Luxembourg. There they made an exact copy of Our Lady of Consolation.
Mr. Rogier brought this statue back, arriving in New York City on July 4,
1867. From there it was transported to Leopold and enshrined on the
side altar of St. Augustine Church.

The statue is an image of Our Blessed Mother holding the boy Jesus
on her arm. Each figure wears a jeweled crown and is clothed in a white
garment with a blue cape. (At Leopold there is now a variety of cloth-

ing in the colors of the liturgical seasons.) Mary holds in her hand a scepter, by which she proclaims her power as Queen of Heaven and Earth. A silver heart is suspended from her arm to show her love for her Divine Son. The long key, with the teeth forming the monogram for *Ave Maria,* symbolizes her ready access to the treasury of God's grace. The Child holds a ball and cross to show his redemption of the world through suffering death.

SHRINE INFORMATION

> Our Lady of Consolation
> St. Augustine Church
> General Delivery
> Leopold, IN 47551
> (812) 843-5143

TOURIST INFORMATION

Restaurant and hotel accommodations can be obtained in Tell City, Indiana, about fourteen miles south of Leopold.

DIRECTIONS TO THE SHRINE

Leopold, Indiana, is located in southern Indiana about midway between Evansville, Indiana, and Louisville, Kentucky. From I-64, take Rte. 37 south for eight miles, then go east on Hwy. 37 for two miles to reach the church.

FOR FIRST-TIME PILGRIMS

Pilgrims can obtain the schedule of specific devotions and Masses from St. Augustine Church. After visiting the Shrine of Our Lady of Consolation at St. Augustine Church, pilgrims may wish to drive twenty miles west of Leopold to St. Meinrad Archabbey, home to 130 Benedictine monks, who recently rededicated their renovated church that contains a shrine dedicated to Our Lady of Einsiedeln.

OF SPECIAL INTEREST

It was the custom some years ago to hold perpetual novena services every Saturday evening at the shrine in St. Augustine Church. Special novena prayers, recitation of the rosary, the reception of Communion, and Benediction of the Blessed Sacrament made up the service. Each year, on the last Sunday of May, devotees of Our Lady of Consolation made a pilgrimage to her shrine in Leopold. Public devotions were held at 2:00 in the afternoon. Changes in life and culture, even in Perry County, have done away with the novena services and the pilgrimage.

A large marble replica of the statue of Our Lady of Consolation is located on the west side of the church as an expression of the love and devotion of Our Blessed Mother's patrons.

Our Lady of Czestochowa
MARYMOUNT CONGREGATIONAL HOME
GARFIELD HEIGHTS, OHIO

The icon of Our Lady of Czestochowa is actually a portrait of the Blessed Mother painted on wood by Saint Luke and has had many miracles attributed to it. According to tradition, the original portrait was lost during the destruction of the Holy City by the Romans in A.D. 72, then found and enshrined in a famous church in Constantinople for five hundred years. During the fourteenth century the portrait made its way to Poland, where it was kept safe from destruction during the attack of the Tartars. However, Poland was in constant danger of attack for more than two hundred years, and the portrait, housed near a Pauline Monastery and Church, was often a target by the attacking forces.

In 1655, when the city of Czestochowa was besieged by Swedish troops and its collapse and destruction seemed inevitable, a handful of soldiers and the prior of the monastery called upon Our Lady for deliverance. As the enemy was forced to retreat, King John Casimir pronounced Our Lady the Queen of the Crown of Poland, and Czestochowa was proclaimed a national sanctuary. Poland's history is filled with accounts of how Our Lady was called upon to intercede during battle on Poland's behalf. In 1925 Pope Pius XI again proclaimed Our Lady of Czestochowa the Queen of the Kingdom of Poland.

PRAYER TO OUR LADY OF CZESTOCHOWA

Holy Mother of Czestochowa, you are full of grace, goodness, and mercy. I consecrate to you all my thoughts, words, and actions—my soul and body. I beseech your blessings and especially prayers for my salvation. Today, I consecrate myself to you, good Mother, totally—with body and soul, amid joy and sufferings—to obtain for myself and others your blessings on this earth and eternal life in heaven. Amen.

ABOUT THE SHRINE

A memorial to Polish independence and a monument to the hope of peace, the Shrine of Our Lady of Czestochowa was dedicated in Garfield Heights, Ohio, on October 1, 1939. The shrine, which is nineteen feet high and twelve feet wide, with a sacristy adjoining it in the rear, is of Byzantine design and buff brick, in keeping with the Provincial Home of the Sisters of St. Joseph. It contains the exact replica of the original world-famous icon of Our Lady of Czestochowa enshrined in the Shrine Church at Jasna Gora in Czestochowa, Poland. The icon sent to Garfield Heights from Jasna Gora, Poland, was painted by a Pauline Father. The Pauline Fathers in Poland blessed the icon and touched it to the original at the shrine before shipment to the United States.

Call it providential, call it strange, but this icon, which was to be exported on a ship leaving Poland, was five minutes late for shipping and missed the boat. That very ship was sunk on its way to America. The next ship, carrying the icon, was the last one out of Poland before the ports were closed because of the war. So on the day of her "expulsion" from Poland, Mary came to Garfield Heights, Ohio.

SHRINE INFORMATION

Sisters of St. Joseph of the Third Order of St. Francis
Marymount Congregational Home
12215 Granger Road
Garfield Heights, OH 44125

TOURIST INFORMATION

Specific information regarding restaurant and hotel accommodations can be obtained by writing to the above address.

DIRECTIONS TO THE SHRINE

Garfield Heights, Ohio, a suburb of the city of Cleveland, is located south of downtown Cleveland. It is best accessed via I-480; take the Granger Road exit west. The shrine is just a few blocks west of the interstate highway on the north side of the street.

OF SPECIAL INTEREST

The original portrait of Our Lady of Czestochowa is that of the Blessed Mother and Child. Because the faces of Mother and Child are black, it was concluded that age and the accumulation of soot had darkened the painting. However, after the painting was restored, the faces remained dark!

✠

Our Lady of the Prairies
CARMELITE NUNS
WAHPETON, NORTH DAKOTA

PRAYER TO OUR LADY OF THE PRAIRIES

Our dearest Mother Mary, behold us, your children, at your feet. We have come to plead for this favor (mention request). We beg you to present our petition to your Divine Son. If you will plead for us, we shall not be refused. We know, dearest Mother, that you want us to seek God's will in all things. Therefore, with childlike trust we abandon ourselves to God's holy will concerning our request. If what we ask for should not be granted, pray that we may receive that which will be of greater benefit to our souls. Our Lady, Queen of the Prairies, hear our prayer. Look upon our

*love for you and the confidence we have in you. Do not refuse us,
sweet Mother, but for the sake of Jesus, your loving son, hear and
grant our prayer. Amen.*

ABOUT THE SHRINE

The statue of Our
Lady of the Prairies was
donated by Mr. and
Mrs. Paul Rahe of
Muncie, Indiana, and
the shrine and stone-
work were a gift of the
Ida Haberman family
of Barney. Mr. Robert J.
Roberts of Moorhead
designed the shrine,
and Br. Stanislaus
Reybitz, O. Carm., built
it with the help of vol-
unteers.

The Wayside Shrine of Our Lady of the Prairies has become a
noted place of pilgrimage in the Midwest. *(Our Lady of the
Prairies)*

SHRINE INFORMATION

Shrine of Our Lady of the Prairies
Carmelite Nuns
17765 78th Street SE
Wahpeton, ND 58075-9310
(701) 235-6429

TOURIST INFORMATION

Restaurant facilities and overnight lodging can be arranged by contacting the Chamber of Commerce at (701) 642-8744.

DIRECTIONS TO THE SHRINE

The Shrine of Our Lady of the Prairies is located on the front grounds
of the Carmelite Nuns cloistered monastery. It is 6.5 miles northwest
of Wahpeton, which is 45 miles south of Fargo. The nearest airport is
in Fargo. Follow I-29 south from Fargo, and take exit 23 for Wahpeton.

FOR FIRST-TIME PILGRIMS

An annual pilgrimage takes place on the Sunday nearest the Assumption, and in recent years it has been linked up with Bishop James S. Sullivan's "Walk with Christ for Life," a peaceful procession of song and prayer leading to North Dakota's only abortion center. The pilgrimage begins with the Eucharistic procession followed by a pilgrimage to the Carmel of Mary Monastery. The cloistered nuns of the monastery host a fifteen-decade rosary for those unable to attend the procession in Fargo. The day ends with a field Mass celebrating the Assumption of Mary and includes a picnic immediately following the Mass.

Individuals or groups may make a pilgrimage at any time.

Shrine Chapel of
Our Lady of Orchard Lake

ORCHARD LAKE, MICHIGAN

The Shrine Chapel of Our Lady of Orchard Lake is situated on the Orchard Lake Schools Campus, 120 acres on the eastern shore of Orchard Lake. The campus has been designated a Michigan Historical Site and placed on the National Register of Historic Sites. The Schools are maintained on the American principle of cultural pluralism, namely, the selection of the very best from the heritage of all groups that make up the American mosaic and

The Shrine Chapel of Our Lady of Orchard Lake features a statue of the Madonna comprised of ten thousand pieces of copper plate and weighing more than three thousand pounds. *(Shrine Chapel of Our Lady of Orchard Lake)*

the preservation of these elements for the future. The Orchard Lake Schools—Sts. Cyril and Methodius Seminary, St. Mary's College, and St. Mary's Preparatory—are three distinct but related institutions serving primarily, but not exclusively, American Catholics of Polish background. The unifying factor among the three schools is their attempt to enrich the American culture with the best of the heritage of the Polish community in the United States. The Shrine Chapel was formally dedicated in 1963 by the late Richard Cardinal Cushing.

PRAYER TO THE BLESSED MOTHER

O Blessed Mother, whose love and protection have kept us faithful to your beloved Son and his Church, spread the mantle of your maternal care over us, fulfill our every need (especially this special favor), and through your intercession with Our Heavenly Father guide us to eternal joy in heaven, through Christ Our Lord. Amen.

ABOUT THE SHRINE

Employing contemporary architectural lines, the Shrine Chapel of Our Lady of Orchard Lake rests on fieldstone buttresses and has giant mahogany beams that soar for fifty feet. The statue of the Madonna that hangs above the main entrance is comprised of ten thousand pieces of copper plate and weighs more than three thousand pounds. It was designed by sculptor Carl Van Duzer. Wood, stone, and glass are used throughout. The laminated curved beams, made of Oregon Douglas fir, sweep to the skies, representing hands folded in prayer. In the sanctuary there is a life-size figure of the crucified Christ in copper, and standing around the main altar are life-size figures of Christ and the apostles at the Last Supper.

SHRINE INFORMATION

Office of the Chancellor
(248) 683-0500
or
Office of Public Relations
Orchard Lake Schools
3535 Indian Trail
Orchard Lake, MI 48324
(248) 683-1750

TOURIST INFORMATION

There are numerous hotels and motels in the area. For specific information, consult directories for lodging in any of the following communities, all within a twenty-minute drive to the shrine: Bloomfield Hills, Birmingham, Farmington Hills, West Bloomfield, or Pontiac.

DIRECTIONS TO THE SHRINE

The Shrine Chapel of Our Lady of Orchard Lake is located twenty-five miles northwest of Detroit and is easily accessible by area expressways. From the Detroit Metropolitan Airport, take I-94 west to I-275 north, to I-696 east. Take the Orchard Lake Road exit north for eight miles. The shrine is about forty-five minutes from the airport.

FOR FIRST-TIME PILGRIMS

The Shrine Chapel is open year-round. Mass is celebrated in English at 11:00 A.M. every Sunday. Mass is celebrated in Polish at 1:00 P.M. on the first Sunday of every month, called "Polish Sunday."

OF SPECIAL INTEREST

Pilgrims to the Shrine Chapel may also wish to visit the Marian Grotto of Our Lady of Lourdes, which faces Orchard Lake and is surrounded by beautiful floral designs. The grotto is modeled after the one in Lourdes, France.

Shrine and Grotto of Our Lady of Lourdes

SISTERS OF THE MOST HOLY TRINITY
EUCLID, OHIO

In 1922, while visiting their mother house in France, the Good Shepherd Sisters visited the world-famous shrine at Lourdes. It was at this time that Mother Mary of St. John Berchmans McGarvey was inspired to erect a similar grotto on the sisters' newly acquired property in Euclid, Ohio. A Dominican priest, Père Ekert, gave the sisters a precise account of the grotto. Before leaving, he also gave them a lasting treasure: a piece of the stone from the rock on which the Blessed Virgin stood when she appeared to Bernadette. This stone given to the sisters was later divided into three parts, two of which are now embedded in the rocks at the grotto in Euclid; the other is found in the reliquary in the gift shop.

After receiving permission from the bishop and substantial monetary contributions from benefactors, the Sisters of the Good Shepherd proceeded with their plan to honor Mary, the Queen of Heaven. The grotto was blessed and dedicated by Most Reverend Bishop Schrembs on Trinity Sunday, May 30, 1926.

PRAYER TO OUR LADY OF LOURDES

O ever Immaculate Virgin, Mother of mercy, health of the sick, refuge of sinners, comfort of the afflicted, you know my wants, my troubles, my sufferings; deign to cast upon me a look of mercy. By appearing in the grotto of Lourdes, you were pleased to make it a privileged sanctuary, whence you dispense your favors, and already many sufferers have obtained the cure of their infirmities, both spiritual and corporal. I come, therefore, with unbounded confidence to implore your maternal intercession. Obtain, O loving Mother, the grant of my request. I will endeavor to imitate your virtues, that I may one day share your glory, and bless you in eternity. Amen.

ABOUT THE SHRINE

The Shrine and Grotto of Our Lady of Lourdes is a copy of the original shrine in Lourdes, France. In 1928 the Grotto was conferred with the title "National American Shrine of Our Lady of Lourdes." Catholics from all parts of the country are encouraged to visit the shrine and honor Our Lady and to place their petitions before her. Hundreds of favors, spiritual and temporal, have been reported as granted.

The shrine is completely surrounded by a six-foot fence and a retaining wall, which enclose attractively landscaped grounds. Inspiring statues, carved from Carrara marble imported from Italy, enhance the area. On a hill to the left of the grotto

The Shrine and Grotto of Our Lady of Lourdes is a copy of the original shrine in Lourdes, France. *(Shrine and Grotto of Our Lady of Lourdes)*

is a large electric cross, which was donated by the Catholic Slovak Ladies of America. The Stations of the Cross have been erected along a winding, shady path, and it is here that pilgrims assemble every Sunday at 3:00 P.M. from May through October to follow along the Way of the Cross.

SHRINE INFORMATION

Sisters of the Most Holy Trinity
21281 Chardon Road
Euclid, OH 44117-1591
(216) 481-8232

TOURIST INFORMATION

The Shrine and Grotto of Our Lady of Lourdes is open every day of the year. It is located ten miles northeast of downtown Cleveland. Restaurants and hotel accommodations are readily available in the nearby area. However, of great importance to the growth of the shrine is the St. Ann Dining Room, which opened for business on the first Sunday of May 1978. Besides adding to the enjoyment of the many visitors to the shrine, the proceeds realized from the dining room have helped fund many of the projects undertaken to improve the grounds and buildings.

Suggestions for hotel accommodations include

- Best Western (Euclid Avenue): (800) 528-1234
- Envoy Inn (Euclid Avenue): (216) 731-2400
- Four Points Hotel (Euclid Avenue): (216) 585-2750
- Hampton Inn (Euclid Avenue): (216) 944-4030
- Plaza Motel (Euclid Avenue): (216) 943-0546
- Quality Inn: (216) 585-0600

DIRECTIONS TO THE SHRINE

The Shrine and Grotto of Our Lady of Lourdes is a suburban shrine and is very easily accessible from freeways in every direction. The shrine is located just off Euclid Avenue on Chardon Road—a main thoroughfare in the greater Cleveland area. The best route to the shrine is I-90, the Lakeland Freeway. The Highland Road exit off of I-90 will intersect Euclid Avenue.

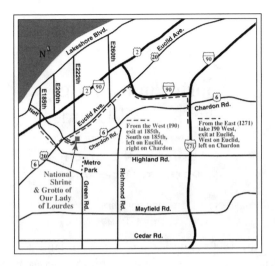

FOR FIRST-TIME PILGRIMS

The Shrine and Grotto of Our Lady of Lourdes is open all year from 7:00 A.M. until dusk. It is located on a beautifully landscaped hillside, resembling the Lourdes Shrine in France. Here, silence and peace invite you to pray and meditate. The official beginning of outdoor services at the grotto, and of the pilgrimage season, is the first Sunday of May.

Mass is celebrated daily year-round at 12:30 P.M. and on Sundays during the pilgrimage season at 8:00 A.M. in the chapel and at 9:30 A.M. in the grotto. Stations of the Cross begin at 3:00 P.M., followed by the rosary procession and Benediction at 4:00 P.M.

Group reservations may be arranged by calling (216) 481-8232.

OF SPECIAL INTEREST

The shrine property borders on the old route of the historic Buffalo Trail (which is now US Rte. 20). The Euclid area, after the Civil War, became known for its prized commodity: grapes of the Concord, Catawba, Niagara, Delaware, and Martha varieties, recognized for their delicious and very distinctive flavor. The shrine was the original "Harms Farm" acquired by Mr. Harms in 1868, on which he proceeded to plant one of the finest vineyards in Euclid. His wife, Julia Harms, was a devout Catholic.

✠

Shrine in Honor of
Our Lady of Lourdes

"THE GROTTO"
ASSUMPTION CHURCH
DETROIT, MICHIGAN

My soul magnifies the Lord, and my spirit rejoices in God my savior!
LUKE 1:46–47

Back in the 1800s America was a mission land. Rev. Amandus Vandendriessche, a native of Belgium, came to America in response to a missionary call and in 1852 became the first resident pastor. Father Vandendriessche was a talented, energetic man with boundless faith

and imagination. In 1876 he visited Lourdes to make his devotions to Our Lady, and he was so inspired that he resolved to build a replica of the Grotto of Lourdes behind his own parish church so that his fellow Americans could worship at an outdoor shrine. Despite many obstacles, the grotto was formally dedicated on May 29, 1881.

On April 30, 1882, Pope Leo XIII signed a proclamation authorizing the shrine for devotions and granted partial and plenary indulgences for all who visited the grotto and prayed for the propagation of the faith. This privilege remains. For a visit to the cemetery, there is granted, under the New Code and the New Norms for Indulgences, a partial indulgence at

The Shrine in Honor of Our Lady of Lourdes has been the site of numerous cures and conversions. *(Shrine in Honor of Our Lady of Lourdes)*

every visit, and a plenary indulgence from the first to the eighth of November.

ABOUT THE SHRINE

Most of the shrine is made of imported limestone. Farmers from all parts of Michigan carried in the huge boulders around the shrine and in the cemetery. Some of the stones and much of the limestone were inscribed with names of dedication that today provide us with a treasure of parish history. In the front of the grotto was a fountain inscribed with the words "Glory to the One Triune God, Now and Forever."

As a result of the shrine's fame, the Church of the Assumption began to be known as Assumption Grotto. On the last Sunday in May and on August 15, crowds of people would visit and attend services. People would even come on foot from the city, just as in Europe. There are still some parishioners who can remember seeing people walking in their stocking feet and even crawling on their knees down the cinder path that led through the middle of the cemetery to the shrine. As a matter of fact, this practice continued into the 1970s. As in Lourdes, God rewarded the faith and devotions of the pilgrims with cures and conversions. People who are in their seventies and eighties today remember seeing crutches and braces in the shrine in those early days. Only a few, however, remain and are housed in a reliquary in the shrine gift shop.

SHRINE INFORMATION

Donna Flax, Shrine Chairwoman
Shrine in Honor of Our Lady of Lourdes
Assumption (Grotto) Church
13770 Gratiot
Detroit, MI 48205
(313) 839-8626

TOURIST INFORMATION

Restaurant and hotel accommodations are easily accessible in the nearby area, including

- Georgian Inn: 31327 Gratiot Avenue, Roseville, MI 48066, (810) 294-0400
- Hampton Inn: 7447 Convention Boulevard, Warren, MI, (810) 977-7270
- Courtyard by Marriott: 30190 Van Dyke, Warren, MI, (810) 751-5777

DIRECTIONS TO THE SHRINE

The Shrine in Honor of Our Lady of Lourdes is located in the northeastern suburbs of Detroit. From Detroit Metropolitan Airport, take I-94 (Detroit Industrial Freeway/Edsel Ford Freeway) east to the Gratiot exit. Turn right on Gratiot for several miles. The church is on the right.

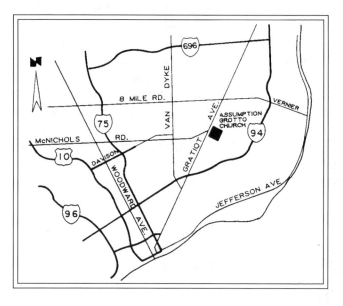

FOR FIRST–TIME PILGRIMS

"The Grotto" is open year-round, and all buildings and the outdoor shrine are accessible to the handicapped. Mass is celebrated in the church weekdays at 7:30 and 8:30 A.M. and 7:00 P.M., on Saturdays at 7:30 and 8:30 A.M. and 4:00 P.M., and on Sundays at 6:30 and 9:30 A.M. and noon. Benediction is celebrated on Sundays at the shrine, weather permitting, following noon Mass during the summer months.

OF SPECIAL INTEREST

Assumption (Grotto) Church is the second oldest church in Detroit and is privileged to have a little bit of Lourdes in the oldest outdoor shrine in Michigan. The parish, more than 160 years old, is a special place, the spiritual home of many who have left as well as those who have stayed. People find solace and comfort there, enlightenment, discipline, and a community of belief. Many years ago "Little Church in the Woods," as it was first known, kept the ancient fire of religion alive as the pioneer families carved their livelihoods out of the thick woods and stubborn fields. Today, the church continues to be a beacon of hope to those who struggle equally hard in the face of modern adversities.

$$+\|+$$
$$+\|+$$

Shrine of Our Lady Comforter of the Afflicted

THE MADONNA OF CSIKSOMLYO
FRANCISCAN FRIARS
YOUNGSTOWN, OHIO

By the end of World War II and the advance of communism, the beloved Madonna of Csiksomlyo, in Transylvania, was sealed in her shrine, and all devotion to her was forbidden. In burying the Madonna in dust and isolation, the communists intended to blot out her memory from the heart

Driven by communism from their homeland in Transylvania, the Franciscan Friars built the Shrine of Our Lady Comforter of the Afflicted in memory of the Madonna of Csiksomlyo. *(Shrine of Our Lady Comforter of the Afflicted)*

of her faithful people. It was then the pledge of these heroic people to their patroness that no amount of dust, no propaganda, no brutal oppression should ever efface her from their hearts—she would always live in their very being.

Many Franciscan Friars, the faithful guardians of the shrine, were driven out of their native land. These friars were homeless until it became possible for them to build a new home in America. They were not permitted to take the beloved Madonna with them. Only in their hearts and souls were they able to transport the Madonna of Csiksomlyo to this new and free land.

Walking in the path of Saint Francis, they came to this country with nothing in hand except their desire to, once again, make the Madonna known and loved. It took many years of hard work before they could start planning for the new shrine. In 1957, through the courtesy and kindness of the bishop of Youngstown, the Most Rev. Emmet M. Walsh, the friars received permission to settle in Youngstown. When it came time to start building, the friars wished to dedicate a shrine to their beloved Madonna, so that through the veneration of the artistic replica of her famous miraculous statue she could continue to shower her patronage, not only over her faithful people, but also upon the people of the land. The idea of a new Csiksomlyo came into reality in Youngstown, Ohio, in 1964.

The bishop of Youngstown approved the new shrine under the title "Our Lady Comforter of the Afflicted" (September 6, 1963) with the solemn blessing of the cornerstone (October 8, 1963). By the end of the year, construction had progressed to the point that the shrine-chapel was opened to the public and the Franciscans occupied the friary. The beautiful sanctuary, with the radiant new statue of the Madonna of Csiksomlyo, was enshrined one year later (1964).

PRAYER TO OUR LADY COMFORTER OF THE AFFLICTED

Immaculate Virgin Mary, Mother of God, obtain tranquility for the holy Church, help and comfort her visible head, the Roman pontiff, grant peace to Christian princes, refreshment in their pains for the holy souls in purgatory, for sinners the forgiveness of their sins, and for the just, perseverance in well doing. Receive us all, our most tender Mother, under your loving and mighty

*protection, that we may be enabled to live holy lives and thus
attain everlasting happiness in heaven. Amen.*

ABOUT THE SHRINE

Inside the church an oratory holds the image of the Divine Mercy
and Pilgrim Statue of the Blessed Virgin of Fátima, donated by the
Servite Friars of Fátima, who are promoting the canonization of the
three visionary children of Fátima.

The main artistic decor of the grounds is the heroic-size statue of
Saint Stephen the King, the first canonized monarch in Christendom
and the first king of Hungary. This statue was the decor of the Hungarian pavilion during the World's Fair in New York in 1939. Because of
the war, it was left behind. A Cleveland millionaire bought it and kept
it in storage. Upon hearing that the Franciscans were building this
shrine, he donated it to them.

Next to the statue is the monument of the 1956 revolution, which
shocked communism in its foundations and started its eventual fall. In
between these two monuments starts the paved trail of an open-air
Stations of the Cross, a unique one called the "Iron Curtain Stations of
the Cross." These stations depict not only the usual and traditional
way but also illustrate the struggle of the Church under communism.

This trail embraces the meadow, called the Cathedral in the Pines.
This place is available for outside Mass; it has a granite altar and can
accommodate one thousand people or more. Over the altar is a structure erected for the image of the Blessed Virgin of Fátima. The bishop
of Fátima had made four replicas of the statue of his cathedral and
sent them out to the four winds; one to the north of Fátima, one east,
one south, and one west. This statue happens to be the west statue. He
donated it to make the graces Mary mediates present on this conti-
nent, too. When the statue was enthroned, the bishop came from Fátima,
and he blessed and dedicated it.

At the lower curve of the trail just opposite the open-air cathedral is
the Shrine Monument to the Unborn. It is intended to be visited by the
people who have experienced the cataclysm of abortion and are now
looking for spiritual healing. The monument was erected by the Knights
of Columbus and dedicated by Bishop Benedict C. Franzetta on June
30, 1996.

SHRINE INFORMATION

Mount Alverna Friary
Franciscan Friars
517 South Belle Vista Avenue
Youngstown, OH 44509
(330) 799-1888

TOURIST INFORMATION

Various restaurants and hotel accommodations are readily available in the area. An outside catering service is available for large groups with prior arrangements. Suggestions for overnight accommodations include

- Knights Inn: (800) 843-5644
- Motel 8: (800) 800-8000
- Days Inn: (330) 758-2371
- Economy Inn: (330) 549-3224
- Comfort Inn: (330) 549-2187

DIRECTIONS TO THE SHRINE

WITHIN YOUNGSTOWN, FROM I-680

If coming from the south, take I-680 to the Belle Vista exit. Make a left turn, go to the light, and make a left turn onto Belle Vista Avenue. If coming from the north, take I-680 to the Belle Vista exit. Make a left turn, go to the T end, and make a right turn onto Belle Vista Avenue.

Then travel straight, and the shrine will be on your left.

FOR FIRST-TIME PILGRIMS

The shrine is open year-round with Sunday and weekday Masses. Holy Hours are offered twice a week, with novena devotions following daily Mass. Devotion to the Divine Mercy is also held each Friday. With prior arrangements, pilgrim groups may experience a Spirituality Day structured and preached by the Franciscans, the Stations of the Cross, the rosary, the litany, or any kind of devotion.

OF SPECIAL INTEREST

The Shrine of Our Lady Comforter of the Afflicted is a commemoration to the struggles of the Hungarian people and the Church under communism.

Shrine of Our Lady of Levocha

VINCENTIAN SISTERS OF CHARITY
BEDFORD, OHIO

The chronicles of Levocha suggest that pilgrimages were made to the Blessed Mother at least seven hundred years ago. The little town of Levocha is located in the southern section of Spis County, Slovakia, and is surrounded by the commanding and beautiful Tatra Mountains. Only a few sources of information can be traced to its beginning so far, but from what is available we know that Our Lady of Levocha, by tradition, is depicted as Our Lady of the Visitation, whose feast was kept on July 2 in the past. Another source indicates that during the Middle Ages a small church was consecrated on top of the hill in memory of the Visitation of the Blessed Mother. A few years later,

The statue at the Shrine of Our Lady of Levocha is a replica of the original statue in Levocha, Slovakia. *(Shrine of Our Lady of Levocha)*

the Carthusians set up a hermitage near the church, and Marian devotions continued until the Protestant Reformation. The statue of Our Lady went into confinement and was venerated obscurely for many years.

The story of her discovery is that Levocha town officials were searching for a valuable document in 1698. In the basement of the town hall they discovered a secret room in which six statues had been concealed for a long time. Five statues were beyond recognition due to deterioration; but the sixth, an image of the Blessed Mother, was as clean as the day it was carved. From this statue emanated a warm glow. Although none of the sources recalling this event tell of the color of the Virgin's clothes, this is possibly the reason for the golden robes and the rays attached to the oval behind her in the Bedford statue. This statue, the Virgin Mary of Levocha, was then placed in St. James Cathedral. One article recognized this cathedral as the first home of Our Lady of Levocha.

Prayer to Our Lady of Levocha

Our Lady of Levocha, dearest Mother, for these many centuries you have been the protectress and Mother of your people. Look down upon us with your eyes of mercy and hear our prayer. Give us consolation in our afflictions, strength in our trials, and light in doubt and darkness. You can help us in our needs and even though it should require a miracle, Jesus will refuse you nothing.

It is true, we are unworthy of your favors because of our sins, but we are your children and you are our Mother. You will not cast us away. We beg you to find in our misery and weakness the very motive for granting our petitions. We love you, dearest Mother of Levocha, and we promise to win others to your love.

Accept us as your children, and cover us with the mantle of your protection. Obtain for us, above all, the grace of a holy life and a happy death. Forsake us not, dear Mother of Levocha, until we are safe in heaven to bless God with you, and sing your praises for all eternity. Amen.

About the Shrine

The significance of this particular shrine is that it is the only shrine of Our Lady of Levocha outside of Levocha, Slovakia. Consequently, thousands of Slovak-Americans have found part of their home, their history, and their heritage here at her shrine in Bedford, Ohio.

An engaging feature of the Bedford statue of Our Lady of Levocha, a replica of the original statue in Levocha, is something not directly part of the statue itself. It is the oval behind it, somewhat larger, around the edge of which are hand-carved roses that form the rosary. Attached to the rosary are long, wooden golden rays and eight child-size angels touching the roses and gazing at Our Lady. It seems apparent that the entire composition—statue with crown and scepter, rosary, angels, and rays emanating from the statue—succeeds in showing Our Lady of Levocha as a replica that has bridged centuries of devotion to the Mother of God. In the Bedford shrine, Our Lady of Levocha is a strikingly beautiful work of art that has combined the historical facts of its existence with the national and artistic instincts of the Slovak people, along with the devotional practice of the rosary that the people love so dearly.

SHRINE INFORMATION

Shrine of Our Lady of Levocha
Vincentian Sisters of Charity
1160 Broadway
Bedford, OH 44146-4523
(216) 232-4755

TOURIST INFORMATION

The Shrine of Our Lady of Levocha does not offer overnight lodging; however, specific information about hotels and motels can be obtained by writing to the above address. Meals are conveniently available at nearby fast-food restaurants, including Kenny King's or Wendy's, all within a two-mile radius of the shrine. Depending on scheduling, sometimes a luncheon can be provided for pilgrim groups of one hundred or more.

DIRECTIONS TO THE SHRINE

Bedford, and the Shrine of Our Lady of Levocha, is on the southeastern outskirts of Cleveland.

FROM CLEVELAND

Take I-271 south to exit 23 (Rte. 14, Broadway). At the exit, bear right to the stop sign and continue to the traffic light. Turn right (west) onto Rte. 14. Stay in the right lane and proceed through the next light. The shrine is a short distance from this point.

FROM AKRON

Take I-77 north to I-271 north to exit 23 (Broadway and Forbes Road). Turn left at the traffic light onto Rte. 14 (Broadway). Proceed through the first two traffic lights. Stay in the right lane and continue through the third light. The shrine is a short distance from this point.

The shrine is located on the left side of Broadway, less than a mile from the exit, but parking is in a large parking lot across from the driveway. For buses and handicapped access, enter the driveway and proceed until you come to a small parking area in front of the building with a bell tower, where shrine visitors can be dropped off. Then proceed to the parking lot across from the driveway.

FOR FIRST-TIME PILGRIMS

Pilgrims are invited to participate in services conducted at the Shrine of Our Lady of Levocha or to make private visits during daylight hours throughout the season. The shrine opens officially on the first Sunday of May and closes on the first Sunday in October. The two largest yearly pilgrimage days are celebrated on July 2 (the traditional Feast of the Visitation) and on July 26 (Saint Anne's Day).

OF SPECIAL INTEREST

Records reveal that miracles occurred at the Shrine of Our Lady of Levocha as early at the sixteenth century. In 1761 Bishop George Barsony proclaimed the statue miraculous, which was confirmed by Bishop Michael Brigido.

Devotion to Our Lady became the focal point of life in Levocha. This continued strongly until the communist takeover in 1949, when devotions declined or were kept on a secret basis. People who participated in Levocha pilgrimages before coming to America give testimony to the strong and loving faith of pilgrims who came by the thousands to visit Mary's shrine. In July 1988 the media reported that 250,000 pilgrims (mostly youth), the largest number ever recorded for devotions on July 2, climbed the steep hill to pay homage to the Mother of God.

Shrine of Our Mother of Perpetual Help

SAINT ALPHONSUS MONASTERY
LIGUORI, MISSOURI

The miraculous picture of Our Mother of Perpetual Help was enshrined in the Church of St. Alphonsus in Rome in 1866. Pope Pius IX commanded the Redemptorist Congregation, custodians of the church, and an international congregation of priests and brothers, to "make our Mother of Perpetual Help known throughout the world." As a result of this command, devotion to our Blessed Mother under the title of Perpetual Help is practiced throughout the world.

Devotion to our Blessed Mother under the title of Perpetual Help is practiced throughout the world. This replica is the central focus of prayer on the grounds of Liguori Publications. *(Shrine of Our Mother of Perpetual Help)*

The Redemptorists of the Denver Province, in the year 1947, founded a publishing house at Liguori, Missouri. Central to this apostolic effort was the establishment of the Archconfraternity of Our Mother of Perpetual Help (which continues to this day) and the publication of a magazine, *Perpetual Help,* which was published for forty-two years. To replace the magazine, the *Perpetual Help Newsletter,* a quarterly publication, was established to promote devotion to Our Mother of Perpetual Help. The Redemptorists of Liguori also offer an assortment of books and pamphlets, pictures and jewelry, and an inspirational videotape for the purpose of fostering devotion to Our Mother of Perpetual Help.

PRAYER TO OUR MOTHER OF PERPETUAL HELP

O Mother of Perpetual Help.
To thee we come, imploring help.
Behold us here from far and near,
to ask of thee, or help to be.
Perpetual Help, we beg of thee,
our souls from sin and sorrow free.
Direct our wandering feet aright,
and be thyself our own true light.
And when this life is over for me,
this last request I ask of thee:
obtain for me in heaven this grace,
to see my God there face to face. Amen.

ABOUT THE SHRINE

From the very beginning of the foundation in Liguori, a picture of Our Mother of Perpetual Help has held a place of honor in the monastery chapel of the priests and brothers and later, with the arrival in 1960 of the Redemptoristines (a contemplative order of Sisters), in the chapel of the Monastery of St. Alphonsus. Devotion to Our Mother of Perpetual Help was actively practiced and fostered.

In 1988 the Saint Clement Health Care Center was erected on the Liguori grounds, and the retired priests and brothers of the Congregation of the Most Holy Redeemer have continued a daily devotional practice in the chapel of the center. However, it was not until 1997, as a result of the fund-raising efforts of the Redemptoristines and with the enthusiastic cooperation of the family of Rev. Patrick Kaler, C.Ss.R. (a Redemptorist who promoted devotion to Our Mother of Perpetual Help throughout his saintly life), that an outdoor shrine was erected. This simple shrine, easily accessed by all visitors for prayer and devotion, is the central focus of the Redemptoristine cemetery, adjoining the monastery grounds.

SHRINE INFORMATION

Our Mother of Perpetual Help Newsletter
One Liguori Drive
Liguori, MO 63057
(314) 464-1093

TOURIST INFORMATION

Hotel accommodations and restaurants are available throughout the local I-55 corridor for every budget and need.

DIRECTIONS TO THE SHRINE

Liguori is approximately twenty-five miles south of the city of St. Louis, off I-55 at exit 185 (Barnhart/Antonia). Visitors to Liguori should proceed south of State Hwy. M on Metropolitan Boulevard for one-third of a mile; the entrance to Liguori is over the crest of the hill and on your right.

FOR FIRST-TIME PILGRIMS

Visitors to the outdoor shrine of Our Mother of Perpetual Help are welcome to linger on the grounds of Liguori and are encouraged to visit the Redemptorist and Redemptoristine cemeteries. A visit to the Redemptoristine chapel is permitted for the purpose of prayer and devotion. The chapels of the Redemptorist monastery and the Saint Clement Health Care Center are not open to the public.

OF SPECIAL INTEREST

Also on the grounds is the headquarters of Liguori Publications. Visitors are welcome at the publication house, and with advanced reservations a tour of the publishing facility can be arranged. For visitors interested in arranging a visit to the publishing house it is necessary to call (314) 464-2500 and request to speak to the Publicity and Promotions Office.

$$+\,|\!|\,+$$
$$+\,|\!|\,+$$

Sorrowful Mother Shrine

MISSIONARIES OF THE PRECIOUS BLOOD
BELLEVUE, OHIO

The Sorrowful Mother Shrine has its roots in the eternal city of Rome where Saint Gaspar del Bufalo, founder of the Society of the Precious Blood, was born, worked, and died. The central theme of the Society of the Precious Blood is to foster a greater appreciation and love for the price that Jesus paid for our salvation. Naturally, Mary, who gave Jesus his life's blood, played a very important part in our redemption. Devotion to the Precious Blood was always closely linked to devotion to the Sorrowful Mother, since Mary suffered so much with her Son, especially during those final hours beneath the cross. She suffered in her soul what Jesus suffered in his body and in union with him offered up herself as a victim for sins.

In 1838 Francis Brunner, a Swiss priest, joined the Society of the Precious Blood. He had been a Trappist in France but was forced into exile by the French revolutionaries. An outstanding trait of Father Brunner was his strong devotion to the Mother of God, instilled in him as a result of numerous pilgrimages with his mother to famous shrines dedicated to Our Lady. On a trip to America in 1838 Father Brunner expressed his great desire to found in America a shrine honoring Mary, to minister to the newly arrived German Catholic farmers in northwest Ohio.

The Sorrowful Mother Shrine is the oldest pilgrimage site dedicated to Mary in the Midwest. *(Sorrowful Mother Shrine)*

In 1850 Father Brunner's dream came true when he oversaw the construction of the Pilgrim Church of the Sorrowful Mother in Ohio. The shrine was constructed entirely of red brick. The image of the Sorrowful Mother was placed above the main altar. Behind the altar there was a little stairway arranged so that pilgrims could climb the stairs to touch the wondrous image of the Virgin and her Son.

Many people over the years have felt the power of Mary. Canes, crutches, and braces that people have left behind at the shrine testify to the conviction of the pilgrims that the Mother of Sorrows through her intercession with God has granted them unique favors in this quiet place where she is honored.

PRAYER TO OUR SORROWFUL MOTHER

Most holy and afflicted Virgin, you stood beneath the cross, sharing the agony of your dying Son; look down with a mother's tenderness and have pity on us who come before you to share your sorrows. We place our requests with filial confidence in the sanctuary of your wounded heart. Present them, we beseech you, on our behalf to Jesus Christ. To whom shall we have recourse in our wants and miseries if not to you. O Mother of Mercy, through the merits of his passion and yours, grant our petitions. Amen. O Mary, Hope of the afflicted, have pity on us!

ABOUT THE SHRINE

The Sorrowful Mother Shrine, an historic holy place, is the oldest pilgrimage site dedicated to Mary in the Midwest. The present chapel, built in 1912 to replace the original shrine chapel that burned to the ground, includes a new image of Mary and Christ, beautiful stained-glass windows, large ceiling paintings, and a bell tower. It rests on 120 unspoiled wooded acres with paved walkways winding among tall and colorful oak trees that lead to the Stations of the Cross and other favorite places of prayer and meditation.

SHRINE INFORMATION

Rev. Donald F. Shea, C.P.P.S., Program Director
4106 North State Route #269
Bellevue, OH 44811
(419) 483-3435

TOURIST INFORMATION

The Sorrowful Mother Shrine is located in northwestern Ohio at the southern edge of the popular Lake Erie Vacationland. Many vacationers, away from their own churches, enjoy the short drive to the shrine to attend Mass. Many excellent motels and restaurants are available in the nearby towns. For local lodging, pilgrims might try the Best Western Motel on E. Main Street in Bellevue: (419) 383-5740.

DIRECTIONS TO THE SHRINE

Bellevue is about forty-five miles southeast of Toledo, about sixty miles west of Cleveland, and about fifteen miles south of Sandusky, which is on Lake Erie. Major highways and the Ohio Turnpike (I-80 and I-90) make travel to the shrine sure and simple.

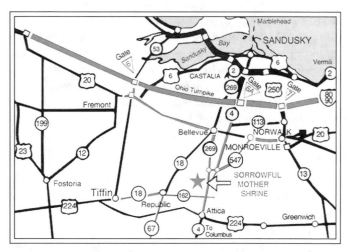

FROM CLEVELAND HOPKINS AIRPORT

Take I-480 west to the Ohio Toll Road (I-80/I-90) to exit 6A, to Ohio #4. Go south eleven miles to the shrine. The drive is about one and a half hours.

FROM TOLEDO

Take I-80/I-90 east to exit 6A to Ohio #4. Go south eleven miles to the shrine.

FROM THE SOUTH

Take Ohio #4 north to #269, then turn left and continue for a half mile to the shrine. The site is nine miles north of Attica.

For First–Time Pilgrims

On Sundays and holy days devout pilgrims, led by the clergy, share their joy and sorrow as they tarry at each sacred grotto along the Way of the Cross. Frequent processions, outdoor Masses, and the old shrine chapel provide devotional experiences that bring pilgrims back again and again. If you feel the need to get in tune with yourself and with God's universe, you'll find that a day or even a few hours spent at Sorrowful Mother Shrine will bring you rich personal and spiritual rewards. Mass, confessions, and devotions are celebrated daily. Counseling, personal conferences, and pilgrimages can all be arranged by calling (419) 483-3435. The gift shop is open year-round, and the cafeteria is open from mid-May to mid-October during the lunch hours.

Of Special Interest

Father Brunner chose the title "Sorrowful Mother" for the shrine because he wished to thank Mary for all the sorrows and sufferings that she endured with her Son in his cruel passion and death. He called on the people to put a greater trust in Our Lady's intercession, in the Mother whose prayers are always heard by her Divine Son.

World Shrine of Our Lady of the Green Scapular
GREEN SCAPULAR CRUSADE
PALMYRA, WISCONSIN

The Green Scapular is a single piece of green felt and braid—with a picture of the Blessed Virgin Mary on one side and, on the other, a blazing heart pierced with a sword, dripping blood, surmounted by a

Our Lady gave the Green Scapular to Sr. Justine Bisqueyburu, promising that it would procure a happy death for those who would wear it. *(World Shrine of Our Lady of the Green Scapular)*

cross, and encircled by the words "Immaculate Heart of Mary, pray for us now and at the hour of our death."

Our Lady gave the Green Scapular to the world on September 8, 1849, the Feast of Her Nativity. On that day Our Blessed Mother appeared to Sr. Justine Bisqueyburu, a French religious of the Daughters of Charity of St. Vincent de Paul, and promised that this new scapular would contribute to the conversion of souls, particularly those who have no faith, and would procure for them a happy death.

Since then, the Green Scapular has become the instrument of a countless number of conversions, plus other extraordinary favors from God for which no one seems to find a human explanation or interpretation: cures, recoveries, peace in families, financial improvements, success in studies, happiness in marriage, and so on.

ACT OF CONSECRATION TO THE IMMACULATE HEART OF MARY

Mary, Virgin most powerful and Mother of mercy, Queen of heaven and refuge of sinners, we consecrate ourselves to your Immaculate Heart. We consecrate to you our being and our entire life: all that we have, all that we love, all that we are. We consecrate to you our bodies, our hearts, our souls, our homes, our families, our country. It is our wish that everything in us, everything around us belongs to you and shares in the benefits of your motherly blessings. And that this consecration may be truly efficacious and lasting, we renew today at your feet, O Mary, the promises of our baptism and first Communion. We pledge ourselves to profess courageously and always the truths of our holy faith, to live as Catholics completely obedient to all directions of the pope and of the bishops in communion with him. We pledge ourselves to keep the commandments of God and of the Church and especially the sanctification of the Lord's day. We pledge ourselves to make a part of our life, as much as we can, the consoling practices of the Catholic religion and especially the reception of holy Communion. We promise you, O glorious Mother of God and tender Mother of Men, to place our whole heart in your service, to hasten and make sure that, through the reign of your Immaculate Heart, the Heart of your Adorable Son will reign in our souls and in every soul, in our beloved country and in the whole universe, on earth as in heaven. Amen.

ABOUT THE SHRINE

The World Shrine of Our Lady of the Green Scapular began humbly in 1950 when the bishop of Madison, Wisconsin, directed an enthusiastic young diocesan priest, Fr. Jerome Mersberger, to begin a new parish in Madison and dedicate it to the Immaculate Heart of Mary. The bishop lovingly tucked a Green Scapular into Father Jerome's hand and encouraged him to promote devotion to Our Lady of the Green Scapular as a practical way of centering public attention on the role of Mary as our intercessor with her Divine Son.

The statue of the Immaculate Heart of Mary was carved by the renowned European artisan José Ferreira Thedim who, himself, had experienced the "miracle of the sun" as a teenager when Our Lord's Mother appeared to the three children at Fátima, Portugal. When Sister Lúcia, the last living visionary of the Fátima apparitions, saw Mr. Thedim's creation, she commented that this statue looked more like the Virgin she has seen than any other.

In addition to the statue, the shrine includes the Stations of the Cross consisting of fourteen stained-glass windows, and all around are murals and stained-glass windows depicting the Holy Mother of God. The vestibule is adorned with the statues of eight saints, which were carved in Oberammergau, Germany.

SHRINE INFORMATION

Green Scapular Crusade
P.O. Drawer B
Palmyra, WI 53156
Visitors for Father Mersberger are requested to call first:
(414) 495-4358.

TOURIST INFORMATION

Palmyra has a population of 1,540, no motels, and three restaurants. Whitewater is eight miles away and has many motels and restaurants. The shrine is easily accessible by car or bus.

DIRECTIONS TO THE SHRINE

Palmyra is about twenty-five miles southwest of Milwaukee.

FROM MILWAUKEE

Leave Milwaukee on I-894/Rte. 15 (toward Beloit). Exit off 15 at F (exit 54: Waukesha/Big Bend), and go right on F for .10 mile to the stop sign. Go left on ES. Proceed 5.7 miles to NN; turn right on NN, cross 83, and go into Eagle. At your only stop sign in Eagle, cross 67 (NN bends to the left, but you proceed straight) and meet 59. Go left on 59 into Palmyra, making no turns in Palmyra, but proceeding straight onto H in the center of town (59 turns to the right). Another .70 mile farther you will pass St. Mary's Church and parking lots. The shrine and museum are one thousand feet farther, also on the left side of the road.

FROM MADISON

Take Hwy. 12/18 east to I-90 toward Chicago. Stay on I-90 to exit 163 (Hwy. 59—Milton/Edgerton). Go right on 59 east about 2.5 miles. Go left on N (there is a sign reading, "U W Whitewater"), crossing Hwy. 26 and proceeding on N into Whitewater. Follow 59 (go left at the first stop sign) through Whitewater and into Palmyra. At the first stop sign in Palmyra (your only stop sign here), turn right. You'll now be on Main Steet and Hwy. H. Proceed on H about a mile, crossing the railroad tracks and passing St. Mary's Church and an apartment building (all on your left). The shrine is next on the left side of the road. Take the second entrance into the shrine.

FOR FIRST–TIME PILGRIMS

The Shrine of Our Lady of the Green Scapular consists of a chapel, a museum, and a gift shop. The museum has four themes: birth of Jesus, crucifixion, Last Supper, and Our Lady. The religious-goods gift shop boasts a fine array of rosaries, statues, pictures, medals, and books, all economically priced. The church itself is acoustically perfect and totally wheelchair accessible. The back of the church is slightly elevated so that everyone can see clearly the holy sacrifice of the Mass.

OF SPECIAL INTEREST

The Green Scapular is required to be blessed by a priest and worn or carried by the person wishing to benefit by it. If, however, a person in need of grace is obstinate, the Green Scapular may be placed secretly inside his or her clothing, home, or possessions, and the giver should say the prayer in his stead. The only prayer necessary is "Immaculate Heart of Mary, pray for us now and at the hour of our death." It may be said many times daily; it should be said at least once each day. Many graces are attached to the scapular, but these graces are more or less great in proportion to the degree of faith and confidence possessed by the Green Scapular user.

Appendix

Litany of Our Blessed Mother

In the process of researching this book, we discovered thousands of places in the United States that honor the Blessed Mother. It was not possible to include every shrine, grotto, abbey, hermitage, and chapel in this book; however, we did feel that a representative listing of such places might be revealing to our readers. We have not included the place names of the shrines that are fully covered in this book.

Each of the listings that follow represents an actual place where a grotto, shrine, picture, or statue of Our Blessed Mother can be found. Place names that are marked with an * exist in more than one location.

- Assumption*
- Ave Maria*
- Immaculate Conception*
- Immaculate Heart*
- Mary Help of Christians*
- Mary House*
- Mary Immaculate*
- Mary Mother of Hope
- Mary Mother of the Church*
- Mary Queen and Mother
- Marycrest*
- Marydale*
- Maryfield*
- Marygrove*
- Maryhaven*
- Maryhill*
- Maryhouse*
- Maryknoll*
- Marylake*
- Maryland*
- Marylawn*
- Marymount*
- Maryvale*
- Maryview*
- Marywood*
- Notre Dame*

In the listing that follows, instead of just reading the names and wondering about the particular places represented, it might be helpful to think of this listing as a holy litany. Read each name and add the prayerful ejaculation "Pray for us!" In this way a simple exercise becomes a powerful prayer petition and blessing.

- Our Lady of the Angels*
- Our Lady of the Assumption*
- Our Lady of the Atonement
- Our Lady of Bethlehem
- Our Lady of Black Rock
- Our Lady of Calvary
- Our Lady of the Cenacle
- Our Lady of Charity*
- Our Lady of Comfort
- Our Lady of Confidence
- Our Lady of Consolation*
- Our Lady of Czestochowa*
- Our Lady of Divine Providence*
- Our Lady of the Elms*
- Our Lady of Fatima*
- Our Lady of Florida*
- Our Lady of Good Counsel*
- Our Lady of Good Voyage
- Our Lady of Grace*
- Our Lady of Guadalupe*
- Our Lady of the Holy Cross*
- Our Lady of Hope*
- Our Lady of Hungary
- Our Lady of Kazan
- Our Lady of the Lake*
- Our Lady of Lavang
- Our Lady of Lebanon
- Our Lady of Levocha
- Our Lady of Life
- Our Lady of Light*
- Our Lady of Lourdes*
- Our Lady of Mattaponi

- Our Lady of Mercy*
- Our Lady of the Mississippi
- Our Lady of Mount Carmel*
- Our Lady of Mount Providence
- Our Lady of Mount Thabor
- Our Lady of the Mountains
- Our Lady of the Most Holy Trinity
- Our Lady of the Mystical Rose
- Our Lady of Nazareth
- Our Lady of the Oaks*
- Our Lady of the Osage Hills
- Our Lady of Peace*
- Our Lady of Perpetual Help*
- Our Lady of the Pines*
- Our Lady of the Prairie
- Our Lady of Princeton
- Our Lady of Prompt Succor*
- Our Lady of Providence*
- Our Lady of the Redwoods
- Our Lady of the Resurrection
- Our Lady of the Rock
- Our Lady of the Rosary*
- Our Lady of Rose Hill
- Our Lady of the Sacred Heart
- Our Lady of Solitude
- Our Lady of the Snows*
- Our Lady of Sorrows*
- Our Lady of the Springs
- Our Lady of Tenderness
- Our Lady of the Valley
- Our Lady of Victory*
- Our Lady of Vietnam
- Our Lady of the Wasatch
- Our Lady of the Waters
- Our Lady of the Way
- Our Lady of Wisdom
- Our Lady of the Woods

Concluding Prayer

O Blessed Mother, Our Lady of the United States. You have been known under many different names. Your sons and daughters have called out to you in prayer and in petition, knowing that you are a loving Mother who cares for her children. Hear us now in our need as we recall the faith of our mothers and fathers who have honored you in so many ways and in so many places. Make holy all those who call upon you and bring each of us closer to your Blessed Son. Amen.

ACKNOWLEDGMENTS

The authors wish to express their gratitude as follows for assistance in collecting information about the shrines included in this book:

Robert J. Lancelotta, Jr., Executive Director, Basilica of the National Shrine of the Assumption of the Blessed Virgin Mary, Baltimore, Maryland

Msgr. Michael J. Bransfield, Rector, Basilica of the National Shrine of the Immaculate Conception, Washington, D.C.

Office of the Director, Basilica of Our Lady of Perpetual Help, Boston, Massachusetts

Rev. Father Pastor, Boatmen's Shrine of Our Lady of the Hudson, Port Ewen, New York

Rev. William J. O'Brien, C.M., Central Association of the Miraculous Medal, Central Shrine of Our Lady of the Miraculous Medal, Philadelphia, Pennsylvania

Msgr. Anthony Dalla Villa, Rector, The Lady Chapel, New York, New York

Rev. Father Director, Lourdes in Litchfield, Litchfield, Connecticut

Madonna, Queen of the Universe National Shrine, East Boston, Massachusetts

Rev. Gennaro J. Sesto, S.D.B., Shrine Coordinator, Marian Shrine, West Haverstraw, New York

Barbara Smith, Staff Assistant, National Blue Army Shrine of the Immaculate Heart of Mary, Washington, New Jersey

Fr. Seraphim Michalenko, M.I.C., Shrine Rector, National Shrine of the Divine Mercy, Stockbridge, Massachusetts

Rev. Harold F. Dagle, National Shrine of Our Lady of Guadalupe, Allentown, Pennsylvania

Dr. Richard Champigny, O.Carm., Director, National Shrine of Our Lady of Mount Carmel, Middletown, New York

Fr. Peter Damian M. Fehlner, F.I., Our Lady of Good Voyage, New Bedford, Massachusetts

Louise M. Cox, Administrative Assistant, Our Lady of the Highway, Little Falls, New Jersey

Rev. Richard DeLillio, O.S.F.S., Our Lady of the Highways, Childs, Maryland

Elizabeth A. Donovan, Director of Public Relations, Our Lady of
Victory Basilica and National Shrine, Lackawanna, New York
Shrine of the Miraculous Icon of Our Lady of Zhyrovytsi, Olyphant,
Pennsylvania
Adhemar S. Deveau, O.M.I., Director-Superior, Shrine of Our Lady
of Grace, Colebrook, New Hampshire
Shrine of Our Lady of Martyrs, Auriesville, New York
Rev. William J. Vigliotta, S.M.M., Director, Shrine of Our Lady of the
Island, Eastport, New York
Shrine of St. Mary, Our Lady of Guadalupe, Kittanning,
Pennsylvania
Carol Srocynski, Cathedral Basilica of the Assumption, Covington,
Kentucky
Shrine of the Immaculate Conception, Atlanta, Georgia
Dom Paschal Baumstein, O.S.B., C.A., Abbey Historian, Grotto and
Pilgrimage Shrine of Our Lady of Lourdes, Belmont, North
Carolina
Sharon Mayer, Major Memorials, Mary, Queen of the Universe
Shrine, Orlando, Florida
Sr. Joan Marie Aycock, O.S.W., Archivist, National Shrine of Our
Lady of Prompt Succor, New Orleans, Louisiana
Julia Tucker, Director of Pilgrimages, Shrine of the Blessed
Sacrament and Monastery of Our Lady of the Angels,
Birmingham, Alabama
Eric Johnson, Assistant Director, Shrine of Our Lady of La Leche, St.
Augustine, Florida
"Lourdes in America," El Santuario de Chimayo, New Mexico
Sr. Alfonsa Bobek, Our Lady of Czestochowa Shrine, San Antonio,
Texas
Br. Gregory M. Atherton, O.S.M., Director of Gift Planning, The
Grotto—National Sanctuary of Our Sorrowful Mother, Portland,
Oregon
Rev. Tim Gallemore, Shrine of Our Lady of Fátima, Laton, California
Br. Joseph Candel, O.F.M., Basilica and National Shrine of Our Lady
of Consolation, Carey, Ohio
The Black Madonna Shrine and Grottoes, Eureka, Missouri
Fr. Robert J. Fox, Spiritual Director, Fátima Family Apostolate,
Alexandria, South Dakota

Rev. David Flanagan, The Grotto, Dickeyville, Wisconsin

Deacon Gerald Streit, Director, Grotto of the Redemption, West Bend, Iowa

Fr. Ignatius Dai, C.M.C., Director of the Shrine, Immaculate Heart of Mary Shrine, Carthage, Missouri

Fr. Herb Essig, Mary Immaculate Queen National Shrine, Lombard, Illinois

Barbara J. Crawford, Director of Communications, Monte Cassino Shrine, St. Meinrad, Indiana

Rev. Maurice Nutt, C.Ss.R., Mother of Perpetual Help Shrine, St. Louis, Missouri

Ronald Lyon, Executive Director, National Shrine of Mary Help of Christians, Hubertus, Wisconsin

National Shrine of Our Lady of Lebanon, North Jackson, Ohio

Rev. Charles F. Shelby, C.M., Director, National Shrine of Our Lady of the Miraculous Medal, Perryville, Missouri

Sr. Pam Pauloski, S.P., Associate Director of Communications, National Shrine of Our Lady of Providence, St. Mary-of-the-Woods, Indiana

Jo Kathmann, Director of Public Relations & Development, National Shrine of Our Lady of the Snows, Belleville, Illinois

Rev. Sean Hoppe, O.S.B., Our Lady of Consolation, Leopold, Indiana

Sr. Dominica, Our Lady Of Czestochowa, Garfield Heights, Ohio

Mother Margaret Mary, O. Carm., Our Lady of the Prairies, Wahpeton, North Dakota

Don Horkey, Director, Office of Public Relations, Shrine Chapel of Our Lady of Orchard Lake, Orchard Lake, Michigan

Sisters of the Most Holy Trinity, Shrine and Grotto of Our Lady of Lourdes, Euclid, Ohio

Donna M. Flax, Shrine Chairman, Grotto and Shrine in Honor of Our Lady of Lourdes, Detroit, Michigan

Rev. Matthew J. Kiss, O.F.M., Guardian, Shrine of Our Lady Comforter of the Afflicted, Youngstown, Ohio

Sr. Mary Gertrude, Shrine Directress, and Sr. Mary Cecilia, Shrine Assistant, Shrine of Our Lady of Levocha, Bedford, Ohio

Sr. Joan Calver, O.Ss.R., Prioress, Shrine of Our Mother of Perpetual Help, Liguori, Missouri

Rev. Robert Kunisch, C.P.P.S., Director, Sorrowful Mother Shrine, Bellevue, Ohio

Rev. Jerome Mersberger, Our Lady of the Green Scapular, Palmyra, Wisconsin

INDEX

ABOUT THE AUTHORS

Theresa Santa Czarnopys and Thomas M. Santa are sister and brother. A science and language-arts teacher at Highlands Middle School in Grand Rapids, Michigan, their hometown, Theresa has an M.A. in Science Education and is the mother of three children. Thomas, a Redemptorist priest, is their favorite uncle; he is also president of Liguori Publications. Author of *Lenten Family Graces* and *"Bless Us, O Lord..."* and editor of *Lord of My Heart, Meditations on the Eucharist, Novena to the Sacred Heart of Jesus,* and *Way of the Cross,* he has a B.A. in Philosophy/Communications, an M.R.E. in Religious Education, and an M.Div. in Theology.

Marian Shrines of the United States is the authors' first collaborative book but most certainly not their first collaborative effort. That would have been when they conspired to arrange a family outing to Gun Lake back in 1960! Little did they know that that first collaboration would eventually lead to this book, and others.